THE
ROAD
SOUTH

THE ROAD SOUTH

An adventure cycling the length of Africa

JAMES BEATTY

The Road South

An adventure cycling the length of Africa

Copyright © 2023 James Beatty

All rights reserved.

No part of this publication may be reproduced, stored in a retrieval system, or transmitted in any form or by any means, electronic, mechanical, photocopying, recording, scanning, or otherwise, without prior written permission of the author.

Cover Design: Emily Hill

Cartographer: Alex Hotchin

Photography: James Beatty & McKenzie Barney

ISBN: 979-8-8704-1945-9

Email:
theroadsouthbook@gmail.com

Instagram:
@theroadsouthbook
@james_beatty

DEDICATIONS

I would like to thank McKenzie for her invaluable support and love.

And to Vicki, Gary, and Kate Beatty.

CONTENTS

	Preface	Pg 1
	Introduction	Pg 3
1	The Wheels in Motion	Pg 7
2	Egypt	Pg 17
3	Sudan	Pg 33
4	Ethiopia	Pg 59
5	Kenya	Pg 71
6	Tanzania	Pg 97
7	Zambia & Zimbabwe	Pg 111
8	Botswana	Pg 129
9	Namibia	Pg 151
10	South Africa	Pg 169

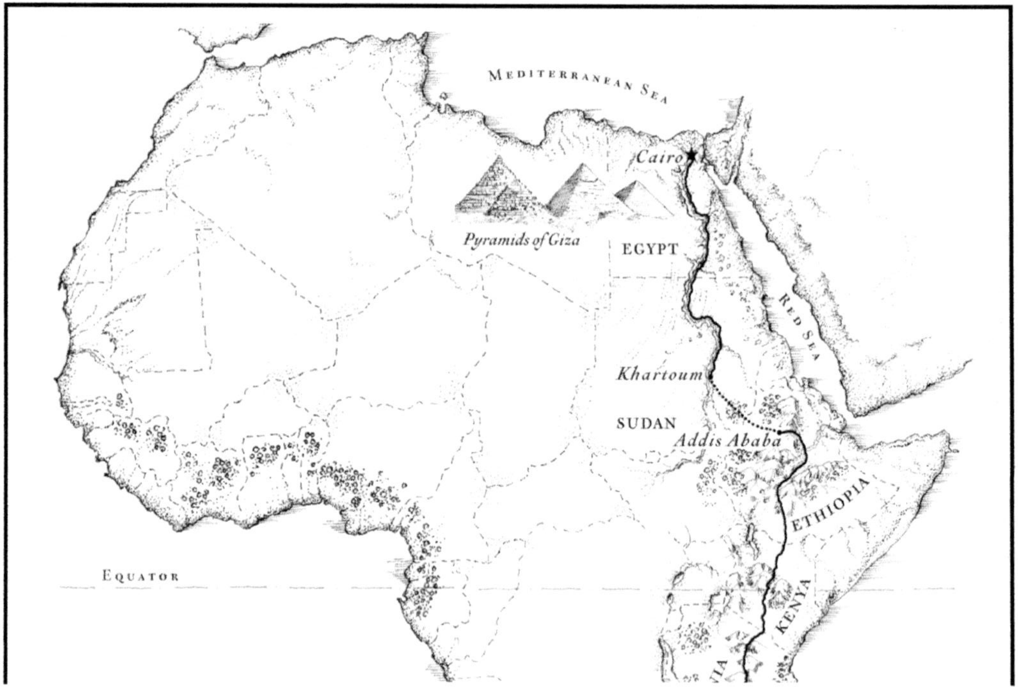
Mediterranean Sea
Cairo
Pyramids of Giza
EGYPT
Red Sea
Khartoum
SUDAN
Addis Ababa
ETHIOPIA
KENYA
Equator

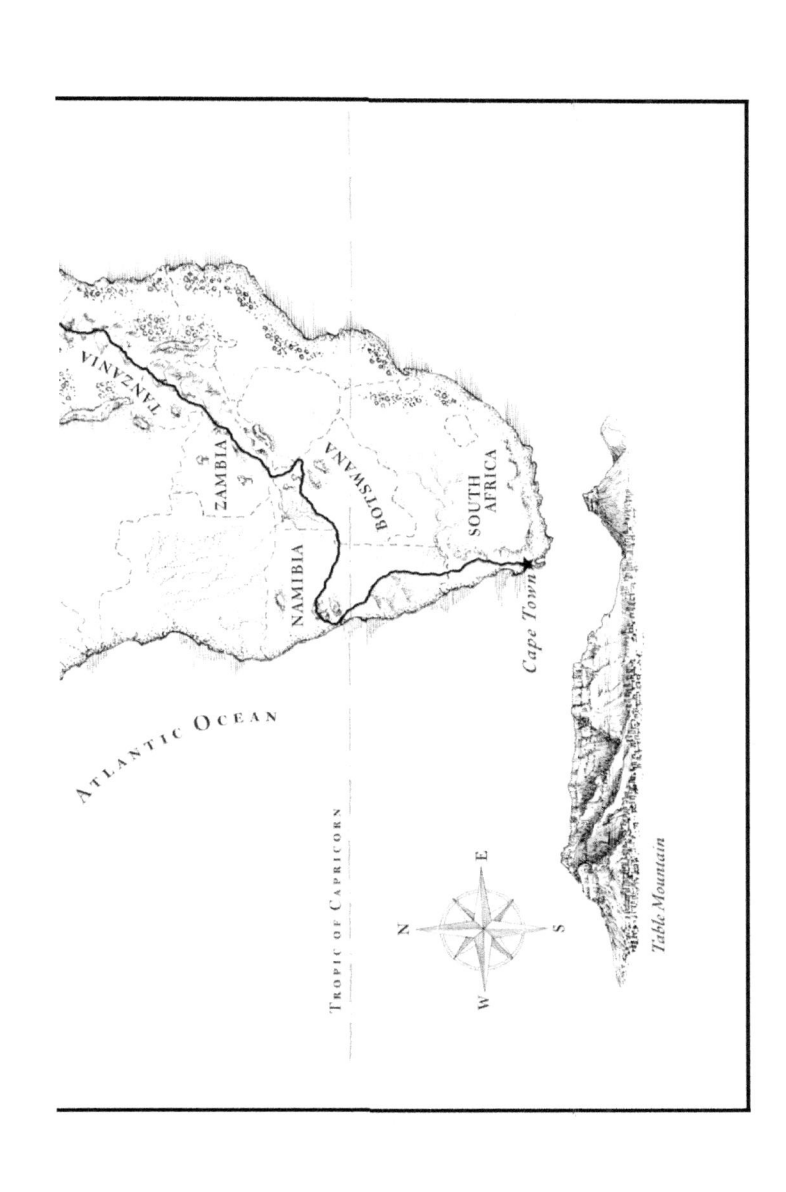

PREFACE

I sit here in a street side cafe in the far-flung corner of a medina in Morocco. It is six weeks until this book is scheduled to come out, and I still need to write the preface to *The Road South*.

What you are holding in your hands is an account of an adventure I took with my partner to cycle down the length of Africa. What lies in these pages is an assortment of memories I gathered by rereading over my old journals and unfolding the large paper maps I carried. From being caught in a military coup in Sudan, navigating around a war in Northern Ethiopia, narrowly dodging a thrown spear in Kenya, and being charged at by a male elephant in Botswana, those six months were nothing short of the adventure we had dreamt of.

When I opened my tattered and mud-stained Moleskin journals to read over what I had written down each night while lying in our tent, I was swept back to the sheer thrill that one can only feel while being in a remote part of Africa. There is a feeling I have tried to describe through a selection of words in this book to transport you over to this vast and wonderful land.

I hope you enjoy this story and one day get to travel to this incredible continent to explore it for yourself.

James

INTRODUCTION

October 2021

I put the key in the door and unlocked my hotel room in the heart of Istanbul, Turkey. My clothes were sun-faded and still had the remnant smell of burnt firewood from the yurt camps high in the Tian Shan Mountain range of Kyrgyzstan. I had just returned from three months of travelling through Central Asia and had 24 hours to relax, recover, and regroup, before my partner McKenzie would arrive and where this African adventure would begin.

At this point, I had been on the road for eight years. You might be asking yourself, *how? Where?*

Why? Well, I'll give a little backstory.

Back at the end of 2012, I had what I like to call an epiphany. I had the same exact dream two nights in a row. It wasn't so much a visual dream, but one of an inner voice saying, *this is it? You're twenty-two, you have a girlfriend, an apartment in the city, you wake up to an alarm and go off to work each morning, come home, empty the dishwasher, make dinner, and repeat it all tomorrow.* The voice during those two dreams just kept echoing*, is this it?* I woke in the morning with a desire to go off and see the world, grasp new cultures, religions, taste diverse cuisines, and sip different cups of coffee.

So, I decided it was set, I packed in my old life, parted ways with my girlfriend, left the apartment, sold the vehicle, bought a backpack, shoved a few pairs of undies, socks, and clothes into the heavy waterproof canvas pack and headed off to see the world. In those eight years, I travelled all over the globe, hitchhiking and camping my way around Europe, Australia, and North America along with backpacking the Gringo Trail through Latin America and the Banana Pancake Trail of Southeast Asia.

My budget over those years is what I refer to as being as thin as a shoestring, which was anywhere from $5 to $20 a day. Living cheaply and seeing the world was what I was madly in love with. There was something so free in carrying what

I needed on my back and witnessing sunrises and sunsets in a new place every few days, drifting between somewhere and nowhere.

I would pick up a little work here and there whenever money would get low. After two to three months of work, I could string the earnings together to last for 12 to 18 months on my frugal travel budget. It did me well not having a large, deep wallet. To scale back what one can spend makes you turn inwards and ask yourself, *what is it that really makes me happy?* So that is how I got here.

Now for my partner, I remember when I first laid eyes on McKenzie in San Jose, the capital city in Costa Rica. She was living there while making wildlife documentaries for National Geographic. I had just finished walking the length of New Zealand and was now travelling through Latin America. I was scruffy, bearded, lean from months of walking, wearing a blue plaid shirt that I had found in a shared house I had stopped to stay in. I was standing on the street and there she was, blonde and blue-eyed, with a smile that knocked any word out of my mind or mouth for what felt like ten minutes. I stood staring, dumbfounded as a dairy cow. I finally managed to string a few sentences together, and we ended up spending a couple of weeks travelling around the country.

McKenzie had moved all over the United

States with her family as a child and once she reached her twenties, had caught the bug to see what else was out there in the world. We shared ideas about wanting to see remote parts of the atlas that might still lay hidden and preserved from the Western world.

After those two weeks, I kept heading in the direction of South America and McKenzie stayed back in Costa Rica to work on her film projects. In the past year, I had strayed away from any relationships on the road. They had not seemed to bring me any luck. Most had wanted to settle, while I had just wanted to keep roaming around the globe. Little did I know then that we would end up travelling the world together and go on some incredible adventures in the years to come.

So here we are, it is October 2021. Months prior, we had both set off from Istanbul. Mac was cycling from Turkey to the Netherlands, and I headed off to tramp through the mountains and deserts of Central Asia.

I'll fill in some of the blanks and questions you might have along the way. But for now, we have to rush to the airport for our flight to Egypt.

CHAPTER 1

Africa changes you forever, like nowhere on Earth. Once you have been there, you will never be the same.

—Brian Jackman

The Wheels in Motion

I could barely keep my eyes open after these past few months trekking in the high mountains of Central Asia, exhausted from the changes in altitude and temperature from Kyrgyzstan and Tajikistan to the sun-scorched deserts of Uzbekistan. Now here I was, sitting on my hotel bed, about to embark on what I later would call a pants-shitting endeavour down the length of Africa on a bicycle.

We had just landed in Cairo. I was scratching my head, thinking, *what the heck have I signed up for?* When Mac had first told me a few years back of her idea to cycle the length of Africa, I had thought to myself, *wow, how great, you'll have a blast*, never actually seeing myself joining her on one of her cycling journeys. Mac had grown up riding bicycles, and it was safe to say she loved them. Her dream was to cycle her way around the world, each year picking somewhere on the map to go off to. In the past three months, she had just ridden from Istanbul, Turkey, up Eastern Europe, through ten countries, and finished in Amsterdam, Netherlands. In a sense, she was warming her body up for what lay ahead in Africa.

I, on the other hand, hadn't ridden a bike for longer than thirty minutes to a cafe on one I would borrow. Let alone, I had not owned one since I was 14 years old. But when Mac asked me again if I would join her, something deep down in me said, *c'mon, you love testing yourself in far-off countries*, and what an unbelievable way to travel the African continent than by bicycle.

Since meeting back in Costa Rica, Mac and I would tend to spend six months travelling together and six months on solo trips. We had been through high mountain passes to dense jungles and barren deserts. We had walked from Mexico to Canada, all over the Himalayas, from the far corners near Pakistan and Tibet, in India, all over Nepal, through Central America and the Andes in South America. All of these journeys were on foot, wearing through the soles of our shoes as each month and thousands of kilometres passed.

Now you are probably thinking to yourself, *six months apart, how does that work?* The time apart came from both of our love for testing ourselves and our comfort levels. I had always treasured travelling solo, moving freely, and pushing my body and mind in some harsh conditions. I think it is important for people to spend time alone to really understand what makes you tick, to be able to push yourself, know what you love, and answer your own questions that pop into your head.

An analogy I have tended to use over the years is that life is similar to sailing your own sailboat around the world. You need to know everything there is on your craft, how to read weather charts, plot coordinates on a map, raise the sail and make repairs when needed. When you get into a relationship, many have a tendency to sell their own sailboat and jump aboard the partner's vessel, sharing the roles. But over the years, the individual forgets how to do certain tasks because their crew mate now does them. I think it's important throughout life to still go out sailing on your own. You must know how to read and plot your own charts and put a reef in the sail when needed.

Before I knew it or had the time to get that wood smell out of my clothes, we were waking up in a dusty guesthouse overlooking the Pyramids of

Giza, Cairo. I can still remember the room, waking up, opening my eyes in one of those moments you find asking yourself, *where the heck am I?* Red velvet curtains pulled over a window that would not close, so the morning prayers echoed into the room before dawn. The place was small and made even smaller by our bike boxes and panniers taking up any spare space there was to be had. We had made it though.

Cairo was dirty, smelly, and loud; a place that oozed with history. It was almost too much to imagine dating back to between 2600 to 2500 BCE. With 10 million people living in this metropolis and another 11 million scattered around the greater part of the city, it is safe to say it's a highly populated and just ever-so-slightly polluted megacity. Now I am not complaining, I have visited cities much worse than Cairo, but from growing up in a small town of 1200 people in New Zealand, it definitely shocks the system. It is the sort of place where you try not to take a deep breath, in case you get carbon monoxide poisoning from all the passing vehicles as you're standing waiting to cross the street.

Those first days exploring Cairo flew by, but now it was time to get serious. We unfolded our maps and started looking at potential routes we could take to follow the Nile south. A map is something that I always carry stuffed deep down in my rucksack. It is true that phones are taking over our lives, and having a map stored on those devices does save room in your pack. But nothing quite beats that old explorer feeling that I get when I pull out a map that's half-tattered with lines and crosses marked where I have been and have yet to get to. I had picked up two maps for Africa, one for the northern section and another covering the southern part of this immense continent. Once we had plotted and worked out the roads that we would take from Cairo heading south, we stocked up on provisions at a nearby market, and then it was time to unbox and assemble our bikes.

It might be best to mention that this bike I was unboxing, I had ordered online while I was in hotel quarantine during that global pandemic that we all seemed to find ourselves stuck in. I had the bike assembled and took it on a ride for three hours, then took it back to the shop and asked them to break it down and box it for the flight to Turkey. *It felt like what a bike should feel like*, I thought. *Bikes are bikes, there isn't much to them.* If you had asked me how many gears mine had at this point, I couldn't have told you. *How to fix a flat tyre?* Yeah, best you don't even ask that question.

We went with a traditional touring setup mixed with a new-age bike-packing approach. My bike had a rear rack with two panniers on the back and I strapped a dry bag on top for any extra provisions needed on long hauls. I had sewn up a frame bag and up front had a handlebar bag that would fit in between my drop bars.

When we travel or go on one of our long walks, we pack light. I normally carry a 30 to 35 litre backpack that I have sewn up myself, a small tarp for a tent, a lightweight quilt for sleeping, and I even cut down my toothbrush. So compared to these previous bare-bone hiking trips, I now stood looking at my spacious panniers, wondering what was going to fill them. I have always found that if you have more space, you will normally pack extra nonsense that you do not always need. We switched out the tarp for a three-person tent, had a cooker, pot, two fold-away bowls, mugs, and a bottle of gas. We divvied up our spare chain links, brake pads, inner tubes, and tools needed to fix the bikes on the fly.

In my handlebar bag, I stuffed anything that I might need during a day of riding, such as sunglasses, patch repair kit, tyre levers, sunscreen, map, and some snacks. In the frame bag, I had a bike lock, a tyre pump, food for breakfast and dinner, and a spare water bottle. In the back rack dry bag, I put anything that I would not really be needing that often, like spare inner tubes along with some children's toys that my mother had bought back in New Zealand for me to hand out to kids along our ride.

In one pannier I had my sleep set up: an inflatable pad, quilt, groundsheet, and half of the tent—with Mac carrying the other half—along with a rain poncho since we would be experiencing a rainy season at some point along the next six months. In the other pannier, I had my spare clothes and some toiletries. I was still carrying that old cut-down toothbrush. So yes, I somehow filled all of those empty bags strapped to my bike.

With our gear organised, we now focused on the current events. Media reports from Africa always seem to keep you on the edge of your seat. Newspapers are full of the gruesome wars in West Africa, incredibly harsh mining conditions in Sierra Leone, and ongoing genocides. Then you have malaria which was killing more people per day than HIV/AIDS. You start to realise that you are just beginning to scratch the surface of the harsh conditions you've just woken up in.

The current situation along the route we were mapping was mild. Through Egypt and Sudan, things were relatively calm. Further south, there was the Tigray War in Northern Ethiopia, which had seen the southern Sudanese border to Ethiopia closed for some time now. We figured we had better not waste energy on the what-ifs and worry about the logistics when we were amongst them. Little did we know that we would find ourselves facing them all too soon.

The bikes were built and panniers packed, all while the population seemed to be doubling around us here in the overloaded megacity of Cairo. There was no better time to get this adventure started.

CHAPTER 2

I existed somewhere between yesterday's memories and tomorrow's expectations. The time allotted by the gods to a sedentary man with a sedentary mind can be too much; and yet, for a seeker, it is never enough.
—James Baldwin

Egypt

Early in the morning on the 7th of October, we rolled our bikes out of the sandy courtyard in Giza, with the dark triangular shapes of the pyramids lying in front of us. With the town still asleep, and the camels and goats slowly waking up, we knew the police checkpoints on the outskirts of town were not yet manned. We smiled at each other, took a photo, and hopped on our saddles.

The morning air felt damp and heavy, with the temperature dropping through the night, causing the air to sit low over the sand. The smell of camel dung hovered around head height. As we rode through the back streets away from the pyramids, the odour of animal shit and urine entered my nostrils. I felt an urge of excitement flood through my veins. Here we were, at the top of the African continent, and our goal was to cycle south to the very bottom of this land mass.

My stomach was filled with nervous butterflies; the feeling of pure freedom was intoxicating. If you have ever chosen to do something that is out of the normal mainstream, then you know this feeling well. You can easily get too caught up in your own life, it seems to engross everything—your job, your hobbies, your pets, your bills. You only get 48 hours back at the end of a week to cram in as much as you can before having to go back to your job. When you push away from that thinking, your bubble of existence widens, and the world lies in front of you, ready to be explored.

To see the excitement on Mac's face was priceless. This was something that she had dreamt of for years. And for me, well I was excited, sure, but at the same time, I was trying to remember when I had last ridden a bike for consecutive days and was thinking how badly my undercarriage would feel tomorrow.

The sun rose as we were on a small, dusty road following the canal on the western shores of the Nile. Villages were waking up and moving their animals for the day of grazing. Mothers were walking out into the fields to start their work and children were coming out into the streets to play.

Here we were in Egypt, one of the birthplaces of civilization from thousands of years ago. I wondered, *were things still the same as back then? Did the sun still look the same as it rose over the fields? Did the morning air smell similar now to how it had back then?*

Being fluent in Arabic might have been handy now, and at any stage throughout the next two countries. But we had both neglected to learn much, if any. Earlier this year, I had picked up a little and could read numbers and knew some basic words from my travels through Iraq. But I soon exhausted what I had learnt and resorted back to being no more than a five-year-old, using my hands to lift an imaginary cup to my mouth and rubbing my belly while asking for two.

We decided after two hours of riding to stop and pick up some chai and chapati. Chai is the word for tea used all over the globe. Here, like in many other Arab countries, they drink it so sweet it leaves you wondering why a lot of northern Africans were not diabetic, considering how many cups they like to consume in a day. I thought to myself, *well hey this isn't too bad. I can ride for two hours, sit, have a cup of tea and some bread, and hop back on the bike and repeat.*

The bike felt heavy. I had never ridden a bike with panniers strapped to it before. It changes how the bike handles and feels while cornering. The gears? Yeah, I was slowly working those out. The seat? Ah, yes, Mac reassured me that after 200 kilometres that thing would feel like a La-Z-Boy... *We shall see,* I thought to myself.

I must mention at this time that Mac's leather Brooks saddle was nicely broken in and moulded to her behind from her tour through Europe. Whereas I had only ridden on my seat once for three hours when I had first purchased the bike. The saddle was as firm as what could only be described as sitting on a piece of roofing iron.

Sore ass cheeks aside, we reached a town in the late afternoon called Beni Suef. We had clocked 100 kilometres so far and my legs were exhausted, so we decided we would try to find somewhere to camp or stay around town. We could not find anywhere close to wild camp since it was so populated along the shores of the Nile. So, we were left to look and ask around for a hotel for the night. After trying to explain to an elderly man that Mac was my wife and not just some stranger I had met on the road who happened to be cycling at the same point on the same route, he still would not give us a room. Outside of the tourist spots, Egypt is fairly strict with its Muslim culture, and sharing a room with a woman whom you are not married to is something frowned upon.

We finally found a decent-looking hotel and wheeled our bikes up into the main lobby while taking our panniers and any loose items from the front handlebar bag up to our room. The heat today was around 40°C. It was only a short day for Mac, with her legs and body well broken into spending a full day in the saddle. As soon as we got up into the room, I dumped my weary body down on the bed and thought, *jeez I have six months of this?*

The next morning, we were on our way out of the town when we were stopped by police. At this point, I realised that we should not have had breakfast and that extra cup of tea. We had forgotten about the police checkpoints and soon found ourselves practising our limited Arabic, answering the officers' questions of, why were we here in their town? Who were we? What did we do for work?

An officer spluttered, "You go back to Cairo."

In something that seemed to go back and forth like a Federer vs. Nadal tennis rally, we finally got to tell them we were cycling—or trying to cycle—the whole length of the continent, in the hopes that one officer might think this was impressive and let us go on our way.

However, the verbal confrontation did not play out the way I had envisioned in my mind once I heard in the thick Arabic, old British accent, "No, you go back to Cairo," followed swiftly by Mac's quick thinking as she mentioned, "What about the train to Luxor?"

The officers talked amongst themselves for a minute and nodded. Relieved, we were not headed back to Cairo. It was a win, in what would be the first of many meetings with police and military on our journey south.

In a sudden change of course, we were now surrounded by 12 policemen, some in uniform and some undercover, all sporting oversized aviator sunglasses and a heavily waxed moustache. They were standing around on the train platform, waiting to put us on the next track bound for Luxor.

In the morning I had prepared myself for a day of riding in the viscous heat, surrounded by the smell of camel dung and the bell-clinking soundtrack of goats being moved by their herdsman. Instead, I was besieged by the aroma of knockoff cologne and catching my reflection in the officer's cheap sunglasses while my ears were overwhelmed with a blaring whistle from another engine leaving the station.

The train was running late. Hours late. Trains in Egypt still run to an aged time schedule, something that was probably drafted up in the 1960s. When the train for Luxor finally pulled up to the platform, we had a mere 30 seconds to locate our carriage and load both bikes aboard, all while navigating through the dozen officers that hovered around us like flies to a fresh turd. We pushed and heaved, and to our amazement, sat down with all our belongings and our bikes lying down just behind us. We had been ushered to sit in the worker's carriage, accompanied by two police officers. They would take turns sitting next to us over the next 12 hours. I'm still not sure if the officer chaperones were for our safety or if they wanted to make sure we got out of their town.

We finally arrived at Luxor station at 2 a.m. the following morning, which was five hours delayed from its scheduled time. Once we had hopped off the train and finished strapping our bags to the bikes, we looked up to notice two new officers standing in front of us. The previous two must have clocked out of their shift, and we now had a fresh pair of deputies to deal with. More of the same questions were demanded. "Who are you?" "Why are you here?" "Where are you going?" Disoriented by the late hour, we rolled our bikes out of the station. To our surprise, the policemen did not follow us once we were on the street. We hopped onto our bikes and cycled away, trying to find a guesthouse that was still open at two in the morning.

While elated that we had made it to Luxor, it did not quite feel the same since we had been placed on a train instead of cycling here. But after being told other cyclists' stories of being turned around at these checkpoints and followed with a police escort all the way back to Cairo, we realised that we had gotten away fairly lightly and were happy we were still heading south.

We had been on enough adventures where you start at A and head towards B to know that sometimes you just have to roll with what gets thrown at you. There were a couple of times on our walk from Mexico up to Canada when we had to leave the forest because of late summer fires raging in the area and hitch around a section of the hiking trail. Sometimes, it's just how it goes.

We spent a couple of days in Luxor, a place that is as majestic as the name sounds. I could not help but think about what this location must have been like thousands of years ago. It had been the capital of what was then known as Upper Egypt and the site of the ancient city of Thebes. Even Alexander the Great was known to have stopped here during his travels.

I looked down at my bike's computer mounted to my handlebars which read: 48°C. It was as hot as a baker's oven. We stopped to find some shade for a moment to try to cool ourselves down. To me, it felt like we must have only been a kilometre or two away from the entrance of hell. My water bottles that were attached to my front forks now contained water hot enough that you could make a cup of tea with them. The midday Saharan heat made it impossible to regulate our body temperature. Self-esteem leaked out of us like air to a punctured tyre. Exhausted, we had no choice but to jump back onto our now skin-scorching leather saddles and continued pedalling.

After leaving Luxor and furthering south on our bicycles, we avoided the police checkpoints as much as possible. On one occasion, a police truck pulled up alongside us, waving to pull over. After acting a bit dumb and gesturing that we did not understand Arabic, the police eventually drove ahead and stopped right in our path, forcing us to halt.

I made it a point to compliment their moustaches, which normally went down fairly well, and then explained that we were just off to the next town. A few times, this strategy worked. Other times it got us a police escort, where they would follow a couple of metres behind our rear tyres. This became our new normal in Egypt and would go on for hours until the police escort had reached their district line, and they would pass us off to the next police post.

At night we would be followed until we found a guesthouse in a local village to stay. Then the officer would kindly ask what time we planned on leaving the following morning. We always obliged, mentioning what time we would be seeing them, and did not fight back. After all, they were just doing their job. This continued all the way until we reached Aswan, a city in the south of Egypt along the banks of the Nile.

We stayed in Aswan for five days, enough time to see the sights nearby, rest my aching legs, and plan for the logistics for entering Sudan and getting our Covid tests required for the border crossing.

After preparing, we headed for Abu Simbel, which would be our last town in Egypt. It had been just two short weeks since we had set off from the ancient pyramids in Cairo. The legs ached, but somehow my undercarriage was slowly getting used to the roofing iron I had as a seat. My mind was getting lost in the possibilities that lay ahead of us. By the time we reached the small village of Abu Simbel off the shores of what is now Lake Nasser, it was evening and the sun had already set.

Once again, we were spotted by police as we entered the village. They asked where we were staying for the night. I quickly pulled out our map and pointed to a guesthouse that I had marked down. They followed us in their vehicle as we rode up to the front gates. We settled on a price with the owner and waved goodbye to our uniformed friends. Our chosen home for the night was rough, but it would do. The antique mattress and dust on the nightstand both looked as though they had been around since the 1970s. In the morning I fixed some minor bike issues before exploring the town.

The only thing that stood now between us and Sudan was Lake Nasser. One of the largest man-made lakes in the world, this reservoir boasts a length of around 480 kilometres and is up to 16 kilometres wide. Further in the north, the building of the Aswan High Dam had created what is now Lake Nasser. There were countless Egyptian and Nubian historical sites that now lay hidden under the water. Certain sites like the ones of Abu Simbel were cut up into blocks, removed, and relocated higher up out of reach from the water's edge. But underneath the water, there remains a site named Buhen, an Egyptian town that dates back to the Old Kingdom era of 2686 - 2181 BCE, on the Sudanese side of the lake.

There were half a dozen lorries waiting for the gates to open and load onto a small ferry that would transport us across Lake Nasser. Grabbing our bikes, we walked them out onto the vessel. The whistle blew as we pulled away from the shore and set off across Lake Nasser on the boat.

Having reached the other side, we wheeled our bikes off the barge as the lorries rushed past. We were now left with just ourselves and the wide-open Sahara Desert. The sun began to set over the vast, expansive horizon. It was quiet, with no trace of any vehicles, buildings, or humans. Just the two of us on our bicycles and the ever-so-slight noise in the far-off distance of sand swirling over top of more sand. At last, this was what Mac and I had both dreamt of when we had thought about cycling through the deserts of Egypt and Sudan. We smiled at each other as the kilometres flew by.

We saw in the distance the line of trucks and the closed gates of the border station. We rode up and waved down a soldier who told us the border was closed for the day and would reopen the next day. After a few minutes, some more soldiers came by, interested in the two white foreigners on bicycles, and allowed us to come into the gated military area. One soldier took our passports and scanned our bags, then told us we could go to one of their cafeterias inside the border post for some food and that we were welcome to spend the night there.

When we entered the cafeteria, the workers were excited to see foreigners and hear some stories from our ride. They cooked up some food, and we spent the night trying to converse with our new Sudanese friends.

We woke in the morning feeling pretty weary, splashed some water on our faces, deflated our blow-up pillows, rolled up our scarves that we had used as a blanket, and went outside to ask an officer what time the border would be opening.

They told us, "Sometime after 11 am." It was only about 7 am and I thought to myself, *why is the border opening so late?*

We walked around and found the same soldier who had taken our passports the night before and asked if he could let us through early. He smiled, handed our passports back and said, "As you wish."

We rolled through no-man's-land, elated that we had completed our first country on the road south. Little did we know what awaited beyond the border.

James Beatty

CHAPTER 3

I've decided I'm going to live this life for some time to come. The freedom and simple beauty is just too good to pass up. —Chris McCandless

Sudan

The Sudanese border post lay in the middle of nowhere. It resembled more of a port that had just offloaded a container ship of supplies sprawled out in the endless sand than a border in the middle of the desert. Approaching the border, we zig-zagged through pallets of cereal, boxes of canned drinks, and sacks filled with sugar and flour. The workers were busy checking over the supplies before reloading them back onto their trucks. We were told to wait our turn to see an immigration officer, so we took a seat in the morning sun just as it was starting to heat up for the day.

While we sat there waiting, I wandered around to find a fixer, hoping to change over some of our remaining Egyptian money into Sudanese pounds. Historically, Sudan has had an ever-increasing inflation rate. This year it was reaching an all-time high. In 2018, Sudan was ranked third highest in the world for currency inflation; only South Sudan and Venezuela sat in a worse position. The mass of notes I was handed in exchange for my Egyptian pounds was overwhelming. I now resembled a kid who had just carved a Halloween pumpkin, holding it in both arms and trying not to break his creation while attempting to walk. I swiftly shoved wads of cash into the pockets of my shorts and shirt and up the cuff of my sleeves. I dashed back to find Mac, trying not to leave a trail of notes for onlookers. With a vague look through our panniers and a stamp in our passports from the officials, we were through immigration.

I love land border crossings in how contrasting they are from arriving in a country by plane. With government budgets attempting to modernise the experience, airports never seem to be an accurate representation of the rest of the country. Everyone is uptight. There are eyes watching, dogs sniffing, and all seem to be in a hurry. Land borders, on the other hand, are much more accommodating. In many areas of the world, they consist of just one or two buildings. Officials tend to be more relaxed. I have lost count of the number of times I have crossed a border and never had my bags looked at. Mostly hassle-free, I exchange a smile for a stamp, and on I walk. Land borders are a glimpse into the past, a way of the world that used to be, a quick introduction, a head nod, and off you go. It is places like these that give you the feeling that nothing drastic has changed after so many years. In today's day and age, everything is transforming rapidly, and technology is evolving faster than we can keep up. It's refreshing to still find the pockets on the globe where your name and documents are still written by hand into a largely bound book instead of scanned into a computer.

Once through the Egypt-Sudan border, we stopped at a small run-down shack that was constructed out of little more than tin and wood from leftover pallets. It resembled more of a shipwreck that had washed up centuries ago than a cafeteria. Without refrigeration available, we opted for a lukewarm beverage and decided to start pedalling.

We were soon in the middle of the desert again. There were no buildings or signs of life, just a wide open road of tarmac under our tyres. The movement of cycling soon became hypnotic. Without distractions to the eyes or mind, we found ourselves slipping away. Miles began to disappear, as hours felt like minutes.

Before long, we came upon the town of Wadi Halfa, which lies on the shores of Lake Nasser. The local Nubian people have inhabited these areas along the edge of the Nile for thousands of years and call this Lake Nubia. The old version of Wadi Halfa was completely destroyed in the making of the Aswan High Dam and now lay under the water. The locals relocated once the water level rose, building what they now refer to as New Halfa.

Over the years, the town of Wadi Halfa became a busy port, shipping goods and soldiers. During World War II, the town was used as a communications post. It used to have a working train station and was a connecting town for passengers and goods being freighted over from Egypt, though now the trains have stopped. The tracks are slowly being taken over by the desert and lay half-hidden in the sand.

Wadi Halfa became our first real glimpse of civilization in Sudan. As we turned off the main road and into the township, we could sense a stark change from Egypt. We counted ourselves fortunate to get to experience a country that does not receive many visitors. We were lucky enough to witness the quaint town going about its day-to-day. It was similar to when you remove the back of an old watch and can sit and appreciate all of the fine craftsmanship. We navigated our way through the sandy roads until we arrived at a guesthouse that looked slightly more appealing than the cinder block shacks using a sheet of roofing iron as a door.

Back at the border, we were given an alien stamp in our passports, which allowed us three days to reach either Wadi Halfa or Khartoum, the capital. Once in Khartoum, we would then have to pay once again to get a one-month visa. The endless amounts of red tape and formalities left me confused.

Back in Cairo, we had waited in a queue of people for six gruelling hours and paid $150 for a Sudanese visa that was glued into our passport. Now we had to register at the police station in Wadi Halfa and pay again for yet another stamp. I could not help but think we were getting taken for a ride.

The next morning, we walked to the station, and yet another amusing day with Sudanese officials began. The police station in Wadi Halfa resembled more of a building site that was either in the early stages of being built or the later stages of being demolished. The concrete walls lay tumbled into piles on the sandy earth. There was a courtyard that had a couple of trees growing—some of the only trees I noticed in the entire town.

Most of the rooms did not have doors apart from the cells. It was hard to tell who an officer was and who had just been let out from a night in lockup. Both seemed to stink of a mixture of booze and urine.

After an exhausting hour, we finally found an officer. He handed us a form and indicated we needed copies of our passports and visa pages. So, we walked out of the rubble and down the street to find a photocopying shop, made a few copies, and went back to the building site.

We were then told we needed even more copies of the stamped pages, not two as we were previously told, but now four. At this stage, I started to think maybe the officer was having a laugh with us.

Once more, we went back to the photocopy shop, and then returned to the station. Again, we answered the familiar questions of who we were and what we were doing in Sudan. After the roundabout logistics, we had our fingerprints stamped on an old ink pad that was probably used by the British back during the war. We waited an hour for an administrative lady to do god-knows-what with our passports and papers. She might have been sending a Morse code to Khartoum for all we knew. We were then pointed back to the chief officer, who finally pulled out the ink pad to stamp our passports.

After the seemingly never-ending bureaucratic nightmare, they handed us our documents back. The officer then pulled out a big bag of dates and offered us some. With a smile, we walked out, hands full of dried fruit and passports completed with the correct stamp to continue south. After a procedure totalling over four excruciating hours, there was nothing to do but laugh.

We woke early the following morning to get a head start before the sun rose over the Nubian Desert. By the middle of the day, temperatures soared to 48°C. Most likely temperatures rose higher than that, but my bike computer had shit itself after being exposed to the scorching heat back in Egypt.

Along the main road in Sudan, we found what locals refer to as 'cafeterias.' They are no more than an open-ended tin or wooden structure with an earthen floor, two sides, and a roof. Inside, we found some bottles of Coca-Cola and either an old man or woman brewing tea—the same sugar-overloaded concoction that, after a few days of drinking, had my taste buds addicted.

Besides the tea, locals normally had a large pot of beans boiling for the Sudanese traditional dish called 'fuul.' Imagine beans boiled for hours, dumped into a bowl, drenched with whatever oil lying around—mostly sunflower or vegetable oil—with some chopped raw onion added in and a pinch of salt. To accompany the dish, you are handed bread in the form of a circular disc-shaped loaf that is light and fluffy, normally a type that is found all over Sudan. You tear it off in chunks and dip it into the oil-laden bean soup. The meal is flavorful, but as it looks in the dish is exactly how it appears, exiting from you at 100 kilometres per hour into the toilet bowl.

You eat purely with your right hand, which is the same in Egypt, the Middle East, and over a good portion of the world. They use the left hand to wipe their behind after the beans come flying out. Needless to say, it is respectful to leave that hand under the table when you eat, and always keep in mind which hand a stranger offers when shaking hello.

Before setting off on these sorts of adventures, it is easy to bog yourself down with the nitty-gritty, the distances, seasons, equipment, and so on, but one thing I have found is that with the right amount of curiosity for the places you're headed, that is what will get you through. Don't get me wrong, the appropriate gear is needed, such as some skill at reading a map and building a fire, but those things are easily taught. Maintaining the excitement and drive to keep pushing yourself is vital when you awake to everything frozen in your tent or are crossing a desert in extreme temperatures and can feel the effects of heat exhaustion coming on faster than a snake bite's venom. Day in and day out, that resilience you build up stays with you. I always find it's the hardest days on any adventure that are the ones that stay with you long after the journey is over.

The wind was blowing from the north, the roads were reasonably flat and delightfully paved. Although my saddle had not yet moulded to my buttocks, my body was slowly breaking into the repetitive motion of cycling day after day.

After making a stop in the morning at a cafeteria, we rode for the rest of the day towards a small village, our destination for the night. Upon reaching the hamlet, we discovered it was far from the welcoming quaint and cosy picture in our minds. It was a miner's camp, set up for the extraction of minerals at a nearby site. Boisterous and wild, there was not a female in sight. As we rode through the camp on both sides of the road, I could not help but notice the hundred or so eyes all staring at Mac. She and I agreed swiftly that we would not be stopping here for the night and hopped back on our bikes, just as some devious-looking characters approached. Hearts racing, we ended up riding another 50 kilometres, totalling what would be our longest day in the saddle of 190 kilometres. Finally, we pulled into the town of Abri just as the sun was dipping in the sky.

Abri lay on the edge of the Nile and was a traditional Nubian village. It had not been altered yet by Western means or mining. We found a local guesthouse that had a piece of paper posted on the front gate saying that because of the lack of tourists from Covid, the guesthouse was now closed. The owner had left his phone number on the piece of paper and luckily, we were able to reach him. He wandered down from his home and opened the guesthouse, allowing us to stay. I was wrecked after 190 kilometres on a loaded touring bicycle. My body was telling me it had had enough for the day.

Once we got settled into a room, it was time for a swim. Now how many people dream of a dip in the Nile? From ancient civilizations, this river had been and continues to be a life source for millions of people.

I stood on the bank and watched the current swirl and flow by at a rapid pace, wondering if the muddy water had ever resembled a clear hue over the years or if it had always been this shit-brown colour. Some will say it's unsafe to take a swim in the Nile, partly because it is home to the Nile crocodile, known to be an aggressive creature from prehistoric times and likes to snack on humans, as well as the bacteria that basks in this brackish liquid ecosystem.

All that aside, I was too bone-tired from heat exhaustion to worry about my odds. I stripped off and plunged in, resembling an Olympic medalist in freestyle, or what I thought. Drifting rather quickly downstream, it dawned on me that crocodiles normally lay in the shallows along the banks, and I now resembled a panicking animal that had just realised it might be being watched from underneath the surface. Scurrying to the bank, I hauled myself out like a pole vaulter, setting a world record. Feeling lucky and that I might have just used up one of my lives, I walked back through the village huts to find Mac at the guesthouse. I casually took a seat next to her and made it sound as though it was a lovely, refreshing swim I had just taken.

We spoke with Magzoub, a local Nubian who farmed in the area and ran the local guesthouse, opening it whenever a tourist made their way up into the north of Sudan. The following day, he invited us to his family's home for lunch and to meet his wife and children.

Leaving Abri, we continued south for a few days until arriving in Dongola. We arrived at a decrepit hotel to see the caretaker sitting amongst a few older men, each of them fixated on the television screen. Across the screen was a red banner in Arabic reading 'BREAKING NEWS' with images of tanks, military in jeeps, soldiers with machine guns, burning buildings, and an abundance of people protesting on the streets.

No one in the lobby spoke any English and the extent of our Arabic only took us as far as ordering cups of tea. I pointed at the screen and asked if the scenes were from the capital of Khartoum. Two of the old men nodded. *Oh shit*, I thought, *that's not good.*

At this point, we were unaware that earlier in the night, the Sudanese military stormed the capital's government building, kidnapping the prime minister along with five other senior figures. We now found ourselves amongst a military coup in an ever-so-slightly unstable country. There were large-scale protests happening in Khartoum. On the first day alone, there were at least ten civilians killed and 140 injured. This wasn't merely a backyard barbecue that went south—we had just found ourselves in the middle of a country that had been riddled with government instability for decades.

The military had cut the phone service to control all information of the latest happenings, so nothing could get out to the rest of the world. They had shut off all television channels apart from one in which they were playing their own reel and repeating some sort of propaganda that we could not understand.

Without internet and phone coverage, we had no way of finding out any information about what was going on. We attempted to translate questions to ask the elderly men downstairs, but none of them really knew what would happen from here. Meanwhile, the military started to occupy each town and set up checkpoints along the roads. We spent the rest of the day in our room, hoping that the phone service would come back on to let our families know what was happening.

The following day was my birthday. We woke up and Mac gave me a birthday card that she had written on a page torn from a book that she was reading. It has got to be one of the most sentimental birthday gifts I have ever been given. We made an extra cup of coffee before wheeling our bikes out onto the dirt road and set off south.

We still had not heard of any new information. The TV continued to report the latest doom and gloom. We figured we would keep cycling south and come up with a plan once we had more information.

By this stage, Sudan's news of a coup had leaked to the rest of the world and was being shown on media platforms in New Zealand and the United States. We had still been unable to make contact with our families via phone, but we could send our GPS coordinates so that they could see we were not held up in the conflict and were continuing our southbound progress.

The days that followed felt like the whole world was standing still. It was just the two of us, our bikes, and the expansive Saharan desert. We would camp out under the star-filled sky each night and stop at the cafeterias during the day for some tea and chapati. Days were hot, upwards of 50°C, and by mid-morning the winds would pick up and zap any moisture that we had restored to our bodies the evening before. With no shade in sight, we had one option, and that was to keep going!

One evening, we came up to a police checkpoint in the middle of the desert. Just beyond it sat eight makeshift cafe stalls. It was something like a western-style highway exit, complete with a lineup of McDonalds, Subway, and gas stations that were all serving the same thing. Sudan's version of this was eight tin and wooden shacks. Each store had laid out seats in rows, carefully sweeping the sand in the front of their hut so smooth and flat that it looked like hardened dirt. There were no females in sight, and once again, all eyes were on Mac. We ate some rice with goat meat, and one of the stall owners graciously lent us his two cots to sleep on for the night. The only problem was that the cots were sprawled out in front of the shops next to the road. Trucks would come by throughout the entire night to get a drink of tea, rest their heads, and then be back on their way. This was just like a Western truck stop, only in the middle of a developing third-world country.

The morning sun rose over the golden sand, laden with plastic debris. Just having spent the night sleeping on cots to keep our bodies off the ground for any potentially harmful scorpions, we had some of that ever-addicting sweetened tea and then I felt nature knocking inside of me. I was, as I like to say, 'well within the warning zone,' scanning around with a desperate look. There was no sign of a water closet in the desert. Not even an area with a hole in the ground to squat over. The tea shop owner merely pointed in the direction of the horizon. He handed me a small pitcher filled with water that had to be no more than 300 millilitres. I thought, *what is this, drinking water for the walk there and back?*

I walked out behind the man's makeshift tea shop and soon realised I had walked straight into a mine zone filled with human shit. There were turds everywhere. Equipped with my sandals, I tipped and toed, trying to dodge any and all of those sundried human logs, in what would have looked like I was dancing to Michael Jackson's *Thriller* by any onlookers. Making it to a safe clearing, I dropped my shorts and took my position. Midway out, I lifted my eyes only to see a man no more than four metres away looking directly at me! He bobbed his head and smiled in what I can only describe as a shit-eating grin. Now I think everyone reading this can picture what that water cup was meant for, but I was going to need far more than this measly 300 millilitres!

On another sun-welding day crossing the Sahara Desert, we could see in the distance the remains of an old building. Once close enough, we could see that it was only the walls that stood erect, but it cast enough shade, and we pulled over to enjoy a moment out of the heat.

Shortly after, two trucks carrying freight from Saudi Arabia pulled over, probably with the same idea as us, as this was the only shade in sight. It was a new age oasis of sorts. The truck drivers were rough-looking. One jumped out and started gathering some small pieces of wood, and the other pulled out pots and pans from a compartment next to his rig's fuel tank. Moments later, one driver smiled and motioned for us to come over. We sat there with two scruffy-looking truck drivers and one of their young helpers. They passed around cups of tea and a bowl of fuul and bread for us, and the kindness at that moment restored a bit of hope I have for mankind.

As the days went by, we were slowly getting closer and closer to Khartoum. We still had not heard much about what was going on in the capital. We had seen enough on the television to know there was still protesting, burning of cars, military tanks, vehicles, and soldiers throughout the city. We chose a Friday to ride into the capital. Fridays were the Muslim religious days when even fighting and protests were put on hold.

As we rode through Omdurman and onto the capital, there was an eerie feeling in the air. The streets were deserted, with road blockades set up on the main route leading into the heart of the city. There were stacks of burning tyres filling the already polluted air with black burning rubber, downed power lines, and toppled poles. Shop fronts had been boarded up with sheets of thin plywood.

Crossing the bridge over both the Blue and White Nile, the only people we saw were military in their tanks and jeeps. I thought about what it must have been like to be a soldier standing there, manning the bridge with your tank parked behind you, turning only to see two white, long-haired foreigners on bicycles. It would've been quite a sight.

Our hearts were pumping as adrenaline swept through our veins. I was riding in front, with the map on my handlebars, weaving through the streets as Mac followed closely behind. We were pedalling as fast as our legs could take us. If we turned down a road that had power lines and poles barricading the way, we would quickly spin around and take an alternate road. Holding our breaths while we cycled past more piles of burning rubber tyres, I thought, *damn, those soldiers could have shot at us at any point, mistaking us for government workers or rebel fighters.* I can only thank our lucky stars. Time felt in that moment to have completely stopped around us. Adrenaline pulsed through every inch of my body's veins and my mind was silently still. I was in pure survival mode. In such a heightened state, I have only felt something similar on a hiking trail many years back, when we found ourselves face to face with a mother bear and her cubs in the forest.

We pulled up to the front of a hotel that I had circled on the map called Half Moon Hotel. We were only two countries into our trans-African journey and facing something neither of us could have ever imagined, weaving through the streets of a black smoke-filled city with tanks and Humvees that scattered the streets. To say we were relieved would be an understatement.

As we gathered ourselves out front of the hotel, the manager opened the doors and told us to quickly come in, followed promptly by, "What the hell are you doing here?!"

The hotel manager told us that the city of Khartoum was unsafe. People were not allowed out on the streets and the police were going around making arrests. Protests were getting violent, and civilians were being beaten and some even killed. After three days holed up in the Khartoum hotel, we had run out of the food supplies we had arrived with.

Peering out from the room's window, the streets were bare. No sign of anyone. At that moment, I saw two people walking out of a door, carrying loaves of bread from what could only have been a store. We decided to head downstairs and walk the road to see if we could get some provisions. To our amazement, we discovered a small local hole-in-the-wall store. The owner had kept it open to help feed the locals in the area during the time of crisis. We bought oats, milk powder, yoghurt, and bread. I enquired if there was any hot tea nearby. He said, "out front," and motioned to continue further down the road to the left.

It was ghostly quiet—the only footsteps we could hear were our own. No cars in sight. Windows and doors were boarded up and, in the distance, you could see and smell the clouds of burning rubber tyres.

We reached the corner and looked left to see an old lady under the camouflage of a tree who had four small plastic children's chairs set up with a table and a little one-burner gas stove connected to a propane bottle. She was brewing a pot of tea. Walking over, we motioned for two cups and took a seat. There were two older gentlemen sitting, sipping on the freshly brewed piping hot chai. The lady smiled as she handed us our cups. We sat back, experiencing what was a truly unique and memorable moment to be having a cuppa.

After the country's prime minister had been kidnapped, there was a heavy military and police presence throughout the streets. Power was still cut. Only moments after our first few sips of tea in the alleyway, two military police rounded the corner on their motorbikes and stopped in front of us. They demanded our passports and an explanation of who we were and why we were there. Looking back, they might have been thinking we were journalists. The military did not want this current affair to be made public, hence why they cut all telecommunications over the country so word would not leak out. The situation was not in our favour. We explained that we did not have our passports or any form of identification in our pockets. Thankfully, the two local men sitting next to us told the police that we were harmless tourists. The two officers, rather annoyed, told us to get back to our hotel and to stay there, otherwise, they would arrest us. We did not have to be told twice. I paid the lady for the cups of tea that we had barely touched, and we hustled back to our hotel.

We spent six days in Khartoum, most of that

time confined to our hotel room. The city's businesses were all boarded up and I could find only a handful of people on the streets, apart from the areas where all the protests were happening.

We would lose power for up to half of each day, turning our room into a sauna and leaving us laying on the beds dripping in sweat. We listened to audiobooks, read, filled in our journals, and played cards. Mac was trying to think of ways of how we could get out of here and whether our African cycling adventure was done. We did not know how long the coup would last, with some coups spanning multiple years. If that was the case, I wasn't all that bothered. We had enough funds to last us for a year or two here in Sudan. We could have bought a little cart and seats and sold cups of tea to locals. In my mind, we had options, and I was enjoying giving my legs and butt a break from cycling.

There was still no internet and only the one television channel being broadcasted that the military occupied. We spent hours each day in the lobby getting to know the other stranded guests—a couple from South Sudan were there visiting a doctor, a man was on business from Dubai, and a local Sudanese teenager was sorting his visa to play basketball on a scholarship in America. Others had travelled or lived overseas and were back to visit their families, now having to wait, along with us, for the airport to be reopened. The military had also taken control over the airport and had their tanks and trucks barricading the runway so that no planes could come or go.

After a week of protests, tension started to subside. Shops were allowed to open during the day, and by this stage, we needed to get some more cash out. In Sudan, everything is still a cash economy. There's no pulling out a bank card and asking if they take a Visa or Mastercard. We went to a bank that had just opened, with cues of people standing out in the street trying to pull their savings out of their accounts. It felt like it was time to leave the country. We waited for hours and managed to withdraw some funds.

The internet was still down, but we found the Ethiopian Airways office and were able to book a flight in person by paying cash. The ticket we had was open-ended with no fixed date. That was left up to the military for when they felt like reopening the airport.

We had the feeling as though things were improving, so we went back to our hotel and started to break our bikes down. We secured three cardboard boxes from a man who sold children's bicycles in the main bazaar. It was all he had available, so we had to make everything fit into the tiny boxes.

Each morning we would take a walk to the airline office and ask the status of the situation, and then would check again in the afternoon. Everything was packed, boxed and taped. We were ready to leave once we had word that the airport had been reopened.

James Beatty

CHAPTER 4

Own only what you can carry with you; know language, know countries, know people. Let your memory be your travel bag.

—Alexander Solzhenitsyn

Ethiopia

The speaker blurted out announcements in Arabic as we sat in the departure terminal at the Khartoum airport, nervously waiting to board our flight to Addis Ababa.

We did not know what was ahead of us. We had just dodged a military coup in Sudan and were now flying over the northern area of Ethiopia, where the Tigray War was unfolding. The conflict started in November 2020 as a civil war between the Ethiopian Federal Government, the Eritrean Defence Force, and the TPLF (Tigray People's Liberation Front). The death toll was increasing each day, with what was reported on worldwide media to reach over 600,000. Hunger and famine were getting worse, with aid trucks carrying supplies being stopped and withheld. To add to it all, in the past few days, the TPLF had started to move south with talks of aiming at the capital Addis Ababa. There was now a call for all US and UN citizens to leave the country.

Our plane landed late in the evening and the sun had long ago set. I am not so much a fan of arriving in a new city in darkness, but sometimes you just cannot avoid it. I can never quite get a good first judgment on a place or my whereabouts. We were keen to get moving south as soon as we could with the rebel fighters closing in on the capital.

When we woke in the morning, we made contact with a Welsh cyclist named Sam who had been cycling around the world for five years. He was only a day or two south of us along his journey, but the news he relayed to us was grim. In the south, guerilla rebels had started to take hold of the roads and were stopping anyone they thought might be a spy or working with the government. Sam had been stopped five times the previous day and was held in makeshift wooden jail cells. The men who detained him were dressed in any camouflaged clothing that they could find. Many had US or UK flags on their garments.

With Sam's deflating news, Mac and I spoke and pored over our map, searching for ways around the situation. Eventually, we came up with another route that might be a little safer than the road Sam had taken.

In ten years of travelling, I held some pride in being able to say that I had never had anything stolen. I had been in the presence of pickpockets before and would notice two or three of them whistle or use a hand signal to each other and then create a circle around their victim. I have even been followed in some not-so-nice areas, but still, I would like to think I have gained a bit of street knowledge over the years on the road and have been able to avoid anything being stolen. Until today, that is. My luck on the great wheel of karma was up.

As Mac and I walked the streets of Addis Ababa toward a supermarket, we noticed a man dressed in a plaid shirt leaning up against a tree. As we walked past him, he hucked a big old loogie across Mac's chest where her fanny pack was hanging, clearly trying to create a distraction to swipe it from her. But she knew better than to stop and just kept walking. This is when I made the mistake in letting a little bit of anger and protection take over me. I stopped and pushed the guy. He then turned passive and apologised, pointing out that there was some snot in my pants. He insisted on cleaning it off. In a swift but delicate move, he slipped my phone out of my right pant pocket and tucked it into his shirtsleeve.

We began to walk away, and it was not until moments later that I realised something must have happened, as we noticed local eyes observing us through tin shacks that lined the street. I reached for my pocket, instinctively knowing at that moment my phone was gone. I had to hand it to the pickpocket—it was smooth, he had done it fast, and I had not felt a thing.

How do you go about finding a new iPhone in Ethiopia? Good question! It is difficult, to say the least. We spent the next day browsing the streets with the help of our Ethiopian hotel manager. He acted as a potential buyer of a new phone and we tagged along as his supposed friends, helping him pick one out. Otherwise, the manager had said, the store owners would charge us double the price, as being a foreigner in Africa is sometimes seen by the locals as being an ATM on foot. I now have been trying hard to get my karma points high enough that I can avoid any more of these altercations.

Just when things could not get any worse, the next day we received alarming footage from another cyclist one day ahead of us. While cycling along the route we had just chosen to take, eight guerilla soldiers stormed out of the forest and stopped him. They were carrying old AK-47s and other machine guns. The video footage showed them demanding the cyclist's passport, and when he refused, they told him to follow them into the forest.

He shouted, "Piss off!" and tried to pedal away. He was smacked with the butt of one of the rifles and proceeded to be beaten up by the rebels. Thankfully, one of them received a radio call from a higher-up that distracted the other soldiers, allowing the cyclist enough time to stand his bike up and quickly escape. It was readily apparent that things had heated up here in Ethiopia and we needed to promptly make a plan to exit the country.

We went to a bus station in Addis and tried to buy a ticket to any town in the far south near the border with Kenya. But we were told they were not running busses at the moment because of the rebel's blockades that were not allowing any vehicles to pass through. It looked like we might be stuck in Ethiopia for a little while.

We checked back at the bus station a couple of days later and were told they would try to send a bus south early the next morning, but they could not guarantee that we would make it to our destination, and we might be turned back. It was a chance we were happy to take with the capital on high alert. Rebels in the north were only 100 kilometres from us now.

The next morning, we were up at 3 a.m. to head to the bus station. Our bikes were still in their boxes from Sudan and were now being stacked on the roof of a small, rusty old taxi. We weaved through the dark and littered streets. Arriving at the bus bay we had to pay an extra fee to the bus driver for allowing our boxes on board. We then huddled onto the bygone, rickety vehicle, cramming in with locals who were waiting to travel further south. The excitement and anticipation were high for what might lie ahead. There was no chance that Mac and I could blend in; we were the only two white foreigners on board the bus. You could say we stood out from the crowd.

Finally, the bus pulled out of the terminal as we sunk ourselves into the seats and breathed out a sigh of relief to have made it out of Addis, considering the news that rebels in the north were still making their way toward the capital.

Two hours into our journey, the bus came to a stop in the middle of the road. I peered out the window, seeing half a dozen men dressed in an arrangement of different military gear from around the world, with pants that looked to belong to a different country than the jacket, carrying battered old automatic firearms.

We soon realised one of the rebel groups that

we had heard of in the south had stopped us, and that the situation down here was now heating up. Everyone was told to get off the bus and to show their ID. I am not entirely sure who or what they were looking for. They held our passports upside down, trying to figure out where we were from.

This was a perfect time to bring out our 'magic letter' as we called it—a one-page letter that Mac had typed up and translated into every country's language that we were passing through. The letter explained who we were, where we were from, what we were aiming to do, and how much we loved their country. We presented this letter to one rebel who looked to be in charge, and it worked perfectly. They gave our passports back and pointed to stand over with the other people from the bus.

By the end of the bus journey to the border, we had been stopped a dozen times, sometimes ordered to pay a bribe, other times they were happy enough with the magic letter. That situation joins a handful of others I have experienced while on the road that I have to wonder, maybe I do have some points saved up on the great wheel of Karma.

We reached the town of Moyale by late afternoon, which sat on the border with another town of the same name lying across in Kenya. The bus pulled over and we quickly had to pull out our bike boxes from underneath before the bus sped off. Within seconds, teenage boys waiting for a chance to make some money surrounded us. Mac went off to try to locate a guesthouse, and I rallied three teenagers to help carry the boxes and bags to where a waving white lady was standing up ahead. As we neared closer, I realised the waving lady was Mac, who had just secured a room at a local guesthouse. Shortly after, we sat in the garden, sipping a bottle of cold beer and letting out a rather nervous laugh of relief for what we had just dodged. We were out of danger and now just mere kilometres from the Kenyan border.

My love and fascination for the world has continued to grow as the years have gone by since I first left New Zealand back in early 2013. When I sprawl out a map of the world or twirl an atlas, I find myself in amazement and wonder at all the contours of mountain ranges and coastlines around this incredible planet. I have read countless books by old-time explorers like Shackleton and Thesiger, and that sparks my mind into high gear for what else is out there to see. Poring over page after page of some of these classics wandering through Tibet, Siberia, Afghanistan, and Antarctica gets me as excited as a 16-year-old going on his or her first date.

The journeys I had taken by foot in the previous years leading up to this African adventure were inspired by the works of Henry Thoreau and John Muir. I craved to cross deserts, rivers, and mountain ranges for months at a time. Those trips have totalled up to nearly 16,000 kilometres of spending entire seasons walking in whatever weather conditions mother nature threw at me. I can only put those adventures down to having been truly character-building.

I recall one instance where Mac and I had just finished crossing the Sierra Nevada Mountain range, summiting the tallest mountain in the Lower 48 United States on our walk from Mexico to Canada. Suddenly, I found myself unable to keep any fluid in my body. As hard as I tried, the liquid kept finding a way through my clenched ass cheeks. I had picked up Giardia—a waterborne parasite—from thinking I was a rugged mountain man and drinking out of puddles and streams. I was lying down, trying to gather strength to keep walking. We pulled out the map to see our exact location in case I needed to get to a hospital and calculated that if we walked 50 kilometres a day for the next three days, it would put us in earshot of a fire service road to set up camp until a vehicle passed by. So for the next 72 hours, unable to eat or keep down any water, I slugged along following Mac's footprints for 150 kilometres until we reached that gravel road and managed to hitch a ride to the nearest town where I could be seen by a doctor.

Now if that isn't a little bit of character-building, then I'm not too sure what is. I think it is good to push ourselves in life. In our current state, most live an existence full of comfort, filled with food, heat, and external entertainment. But why not remove those things for a period, push yourself physically and mentally, and meet face-to-face with some of your fears and dark thoughts. We all have those frightening beliefs in the far crevices of our mind yet choose not to sit down for a cup of tea with them.

CHAPTER 5

I would rather own little and see the world than own the world and see little of it.
—Alexander Sattler

Kenya

Ethiopia felt like a whirlwind. In those past few weeks alone, it had shown us how turbulent the continent could be with its political instability. In just one day, things had changed drastically. For the local people, this was their lives, they had to deal with issues arising throughout any given year. We were just two foreigners on bicycles passing through, witnessing the events unfold. Famine, wars, and political unrest were prevalent on this continent.

Eager to cross into Kenya, we rebuilt the bikes and loaded our panniers. The border crossing was simple, the only hiccup being that our Covid test results were slightly outdated. Luckily, the official allowed the detail to go unnoticed. We had heard stories of other travellers paying their way into countries to avoid testing logistics and were fortunate to avoid any confrontation with our expired test.

I enjoy countries where a handshake system is still around. It's a glimpse into the past, a way of doing business that no longer exists. Border control conversations with another human are much more personable than being just another number scanned in by a computer. In Western countries, the essence of haggling and bartering has all but ended.

As we passed through the first village in northern Kenya, Mac and I realised that we were approaching the version of Africa that we had both envisioned before the trip. The sun was an ever-glowing gold, the earth a burnt red, and the roads bare, lined only with baboons, camels, and their herdsmen. We had entered the Turbi Desert and soon came to know why the locals had given the area this name. In the local Samburu language, Turbi means windy. Sure enough, we soon realised just how windy this place gets.

We rose just as the morning light was peeking up over the horizon and were welcomed by an odd calmness, the ghostly feeling when you can sense something is coming. I felt like a sailor out on the sea in the unnatural calm before a storm hit. We had about half an hour to take the tent down, load our panniers, and fill our stomachs with something to sustain us for hours of battling on the bike. All of this before the wind kicked in. *And when it kicks in, it damn near blows your foreskin off!*

One day, we were making progress as slow as decomposing plastic, with a side wind so strong that if you stopped pedalling, you had about two seconds until the bike came to a complete standstill. I had been using a building in the distance as my gauge to remind myself that we were still making a forward passage. Seconds later, the roof of the building had been ripped off and blown across the desert like a gigantic tin tumbleweed. After days of this howling force, you wouldn't think there was any wind left, but it turns out that Mother Nature's wind factory has an endless supply.

The wildlife was becoming more apparent; each day we would see ostriches, warthogs, baboons, and some spectacular bird life. We were nearing a town called Marsabit that sat on top of an ancient volcano. Before tackling the huge incline that lurked in the distance, we decided we would call it for the day and leave the climb for tomorrow.

Peeling off the windswept road, we heaved our bikes along an old dried-up river bed until we found a divot under an Acacia tree that would give us some privacy from any passing vehicles during the night. The wind had smashed us all day, blowing gusts of up to 100 kilometres per hour. We were dog-tired. We fought the wind while trying to set the tent up, being careful not to rip the thin nylon walls or have it blown out of our hands. After we had erected the tent and rolled out our sleeping bags, the sun was just about to dip below the horizon. As soon as the sun set, the wind stopped almost immediately, as if someone in the wind factory had flicked the off switch before they left for the night.

We were gifted an incredible evening; the stars filled the dark African sky, and there was not a breath of wind, no humans or animals. It felt like we had Kenya all to ourselves. In a world that is so populated, it's becoming a rare occasion to find oneself alone in such complete silence.

Throughout Northern Kenya live the Samburu people, a semi-nomadic tribe who tend to pack up and move every few weeks, mainly herding cattle, sheep goats, and camels. We had been seeing a number of these nomadic herdsmen while riding through this windswept, barren land.

At first glance of no human or structure in sight, we would then suddenly see one or two

Samburu with their signature red cloth draped over them, carrying a machete, spear, or stick in hand. They would run out from the bushes, hands held out, demanding, "water, food, money!" The only other words of English they had been taught or picked up were, "give me!"

It was puzzling to think that even in the far-off corners well away from any town or city, you could still find the effects of what I could only think is caused by foreign aid here in Africa.

The day started like many others; we cold-soaked rolled oats mixed with milk powder and raisins and sipped down some instant coffee. We packed the tent and sleeping gear into the panniers and took one last look at our map for what the day's ride entailed.

It was around noon when we spotted a tribe of goats up ahead on the side of the road with two ladies herding them north. We waved and said hello and kept riding. Shortly thereafter, we both spotted on our left-hand side a tribal teenage boy. He was dressed in the traditional Samburu red cloth wrapped around his waist, beaded necklaces, and had a spear in his hand. That is all I registered from the brief glance I gave his way.

A split second later, we heard the hair-raising clink of metal hitting the ground. I turned around to see the five-foot spear—a handmade metal blade fastened to a wooden stick that the boy had been holding, now lying an inch from Mac's rear tyre. The look on Mac's face was filled with terror.

I yelled, "GO!" and started cycling as fast as I could. It had all happened in a nanosecond. The adrenaline was pumping; my body filled with rage, heart racing, our already fatigued muscles cranked into high gear as we pushed down on our pedals as fast as we could to put distance between us and the teenager wielding his spear.

After cycling for another three or four kilometres, we stopped to allow our heart rates settle and talk about what a pants-shitting experience that had been. For the rest of the day, we cycled on high alert. Eventually, we found a rundown guesthouse to take a shower and spend the night in.

We woke the next morning with massive bags under our eyes. It is amazing what one night in a hot, stuffy room, a crammed single bed, and a few dozen mosquitoes can do for your energy levels. As I rolled over, I noticed that Mac wasn't beside me on the bed. Instead, she was lying on the tiled floor where she had slept for the night. The tiles gave the ever-so-slight edge of coolness there was to be had in the airless, balmy room.

We took our time in the morning, making an extra cup of coffee and mixing some more of the instant brown powder into our oatmeal and milk. We sat reflecting on what had happened yesterday in utter shock and amazement. *What would've happened if the boy's aim was a little better, and the spear had struck one of us,* we thought. In retrospect, if he wanted to cause harm, I am sure he could have hit one of us. I think it was more of a scare tactic that he was going for. It sure worked. I now had some skid marks lining the inside of my shorts that would hide there for days.

By the afternoon, our exhaustion was starting to show as we were underway on a mammoth uphill climb at the foot of Mount Kenya. In our lowest granny gear, we slowly worked our way up the forever ascending mountain. Heavy lorries would creep past us while we clung to the narrow shoulder. Finally arriving at the top of the hill, we spotted a cafe perched there, as if it were out of a movie scene.

The weather had changed, almost instantly away from the heat of the desert. There were now clouds, pine trees, and an icy wind blowing. It was as if we had been transported to some little cottage town in England. There were a few farms in the area run by some foreign expats. One of the families owned the cafe that sat atop the hill and had designed it similar to what you would find in New Zealand or England. It was like a tiny oasis for a night; there was no begging, badgering, or people yelling out, "hey mzungu"—a word that we had been told originally meant 'aimless wanderer,' and was given to early explorers and missionaries who ventured to this continent. Quite a fitting name, I had thought, though the delivery was usually given with a derogatory meaning of white-skinned man. We had only just begun to hear this Swahili word in Kenya but would continue to hear it being yelled out for months to come.

This was a welcomed break for the night. We set up the tent on the lawn out the back of the cafe amongst the flower gardens. We spent the evening hanging out with the local Kenyan workers who also lived on the premises, laughing and joking while sharing stories. No one asked for anything— it was a unique feeling, differing from what we had felt so far in Kenya.

As many of you reading this I am sure have set up a tent before, or at least tried to, doing so with a partner is always amusing for someone passing by. After spending more nights under a nylon rain fly and bug netting than in four solid walls, Mac and I have mastered the setting up and taking down of a tent. As I unfolded the Tyvek ground cover, Mac unravelled the inner tent, connected the poles, and clipped in. With the base of the tent pegged down, the rain fly was thrown over if it was necessary. It was simple and quick. We did all of this without talking, a fluid act of building our home for the night that we had done so many evenings before and would continue for many more to come.

The ride down from the hilltop the following morning was exhilarating; the scent of pine wafted up my nostrils and the fresh air was cool enough that it made our noses drip. I did not turn my pedals for upwards of 15 kilometres and enjoyed the delicious, downhill momentum.

Next up, we were aiming for Nanyuki. The line of the equator crosses just south of the township and, as we whizzed through the town, we stopped to take some photos of the anti-climactic hand-painted sign that marked our official crossing into the Southern Hemisphere.

The capital of Kenya was our next destination. The name Nairobi is derived from the Maasai phrase 'Enkare Nairobi,' which translates to 'place of cool waters' referring to the Nairobi River that flows through the city, resembling the Nile with the ever-eye-catching murky brown colour. At the turn of the 19th century, the city of Nairobi was founded by the British during Kenya's colonial days. It was formed as a rail depot and grew so rapidly in size that it soon replaced Mombasa as the capital of the country. These days, the population in Nairobi has reached around 4.5 million people and shows no signs of slowing down.

The day we reached Nairobi is one that is forever etched into my memory. Caught in the middle of rush hour traffic on a busy Friday afternoon, we found ourselves attempting to cycle from one end of the city to the opposite end. Now if you have travelled anywhere outside of a Western country, then you'll know traffic doesn't quite run in the same organised manner as it does in the West. The saying 'dominate, don't hesitate' has always rung loud in the back of my mind, especially here. We dodged, swerved, and swore, having more near misses during those couple of hours than any other during our whole time in Africa. We had buses merge over into our lane, nearly colliding with the big metal whale, only to have the driver jump on the brakes to let a passenger disembark, just seconds after cutting us off. The fumes from the traffic and the sounds of engines and car horns were so intoxicating that it was hard to put it into words. Imagine you're in one of those human mazes; you've been handed a pair of noise-cancelling headphones, playing some dizzying loud music, and the entire time while navigating through the maze you have objects flying out in front of you. In our case, these were buses, motorbikes, trucks, and cars, coupled with a carbon monoxide exhaust blowing into our faces for two excruciating hours. By the time we found the guesthouse that we had been aiming for, we were utterly bone-tired with our hands shaking, dripping in sweat, clothes covered in fume residue, and a mind that was wired to every sound and movement.

We planned to stay in Nairobi for three days to make a few small repairs. I had to replace my gear shifter cable, and we put a new chain on Mac's bike. We explored the city and then headed out to the famous Maasai Mara for a safari. We decided we would take the bus, leaving our bikes behind at the guesthouse for a couple of days. There were not many people on the bus and the locals who were on board stared our way, wondering what we were doing. Most were local Maasai who had moved away from the rural areas to live and try to earn money in the city. We rode the rickety bus to Narok, and from there we stuffed ourselves into a shared taxi with some other Maasai headed for Sekenani, a small village on the outskirts of the Mara. We had goats crammed into the car, with babies and young children filling the gaps where an adult couldn't fit, and we were ready to go. Everyone wanted to know what these two crazy mzungus were doing and why we were not taking a private vehicle. We got off at the end of the road, in the small Maasai village that sits at one entrance to the famous Maasai Mara National Reserve. We waved goodbye to our new friends, after having shared an intimate two hours with them, and walked to see if we could find somewhere to stay for the night.

The town does not get too many tourists coming to stay outside of the park. Most visitors we found would pay to stay inside the reserve or make the trip back to the capital. Some guesthouses we found looked to have been closed for some time.

We walked through an old buckled wooden gate and yelled out, "Hello?!" A nearby farmer saw a business opportunity and came over. We asked if we could stay for the night, and he told us that the owner was away but that he knew where the keys were kept. The only thing was that we had to pay the farmer directly. How canny. It was not much, just a tin shack with plywood walls and two soft foam mattresses on a wooden frame. We thought *this would do the trick for two nights.* So, we gave some money to the old farmer, and he handed over the keys to the place.

The following morning, just before the sun rose, we met Moses, a local Maasai who spent his days herding cows to nearby areas to graze for the day. The Welsh cyclist, Sam, had passed through here the week before and met Moses, who took him around the park, passing along his contact to us for our visit.

Moses picked us up in his brother's Land Cruiser that he had borrowed, and we entered one of the most famous safari parks in the world. Most companies charge somewhere around $300 a day for a safari. Moses was asking $50, and to us, it felt like our money was going to his family and the local economy more than a large international tour company that comes from Nairobi each day. The day was magical, seeing all of what is referred to as the 'big five' wildlife in their natural habitat was spectacular.

We spent two incredible nights in Sekenani and then made our way back to the capital. Loading up our bags and panniers, we rolled our bikes out to the street early in the morning to start our last stretch of Kenya.

James Beatty

The Pyramids of Giza, Cairo, Egypt

Sitting back to enjoy a cup of chai on our first day, Egypt

Moments after crossing Lake Nasser, Sudan

The day we found out the military had taken over the government, Sudan

Sudanese locals at a makeshift truck stop, Sudan

Contemplating why my saddle was not softer, Kenya

Camping under an Acacia tree, Northern Kenya

Seeking shade and a cold drink, Northern Kenya

Crossing the Equator in Nanyuki, Kenya

Racing a local boy, Tanzania

Road conditions, Zambia

Local mud house with a thatched roof, Zambia

Our first taste of Elephant Highway, Botswana

Breakfast while waiting to cross into Namibia

Exploring the salt pan and dunes of Deadvlei, Nambia

Mac and I riding near the South African border

11,000km and 6 months later we had reached Cape Town

Our ride was complete Cape Town, South Africa

James Beatty

CHAPTER 6

If I have ever seen magic, it has been in Africa.
—John Hemingway

Tanzania

I read once that a good living versus the life you want to live is a hard choice that we all have to make and try not to regret. Time is what we are all given when we are born, no matter our race, religion, sect, or gender. We are all provided the same amount—24 hours in the day—day in and day out. Now most of us choose to exchange that time for money, and fair enough; it's hard to find places in this world where you don't need money. Trust me, I've spent the last decade looking for it. However, too many people are trading in too much of their precious time, hoping that they'll be able to buy it back later in life. From what I have seen, that's a one-sided gamble, with the odds stacked against you. Before people get bogged down into making bank loan repayments, think about what it is you really want to be doing with your limited time. After all, you cannot buy it back, so choose wisely.

Moments after crossing the border into Tanzania, it felt as if we had cycled into a friendly, gayful bliss. We did not know it at the time, but this feeling was the beauty of Tanzania; people were often smiling and waving, and no one was yelling out, "Hey mzungu, give me money!" Women were wearing brightly coloured dresses filled with vibrant yellows, greens, and blues. It felt like everyone was stopping to wave at us as we pedalled past.

After crossing the border, we rolled through villages until it was late afternoon and could see a storm brewing on the horizon. Now was the time to find somewhere to set up camp before the gale hit. In this northern area of Tanzania, there seemed to be a lot of Maasai herdsmen roaming the land with their goats and other animals, grazing them on any pieces of grass or shrub in this barren land. It was difficult to locate somewhere to set up camp out of sight from any herdsmen.

We spotted a mud brick and wooden structure in the distance that had a bowed timber cross fixed to the roof. *A church,* I thought, *that'll work as a shelter.* There were a few other adobe homes scattered around the church, so we peeled off the road and pushed our bikes up to one of the shacks, noticing a handful of children playing out front. There were three teenage girls inside the home, and we asked if we could set up our tent for the night while pointing out the storm rolling in. Their faces read a look of utter puzzlement. They could not speak a lick of English; let alone they had probably never seen a mzungu up close before. They looked at our hands, faces, hair, and noses—you name it, we were being thoroughly surveyed.

After exchanging some sign language, we figured that they were telling us to wait for the pastor. We sat patiently while the girls kept examining our features. No pastor came. It was at this time that I remembered I had a bunch of inflatable balls, some small yo-yos, and other children's toys in my rear dry bag on the bike.

I went and fetched one of the blow-up balls and inflated it with my bike pump. We started passing it back and forth between the girls and the younger children. The look of pure amazement on everyone's faces was a priceless moment that I will retain for the rest of my life. Within no time, we had fifteen kids all joining in on the fun. They each wore an enormous smile, and we even had some of the older women who had been out gathering the goats stop by and join in.

After an hour, just as the storm clouds were about to be overhead, a young 19-year-old boy turned up. Julian was the pastor's son and spoke a little English. We asked if we could sleep in the church for the night, to which he nodded his approval. Shortly after, we were inside the makeshift church, which was no more than a wooden beamed structure with some sheets of tin laid over the top for a roof. All the children gathered around, peering through the windows and the gaps in the wooden planks that formed the door. We set up the tent inside, and shortly after, the storm struck. The winds picked up and were gusting so strong that I thought the tin sheets might blow off, just like the roof that we had seen in the Turbi Desert.

The next morning was calm as we left the church and waved goodbye to the little kids, leaving behind some of the toys from my dry bag.

We were on our way to Arusha, the town that marked the halfway point on our crossing from Egypt to South Africa, as the crow flies. As we approached the signpost, I was excited to have made it here. The last few weeks had been less of navigating through military coups and countries at war, and more of what we had envisioned a cycle journey to be. Our days consisted of waking up, breaking camp, cycling, eating, hydrating, cycling some more, setting up the tent, sleeping, and repeating it all tomorrow.

While the body was properly broken in at this point, it was safe to say we were both becoming weary. After four to five days, our legs would be aching for a break. That leather saddle that felt like a piece of roofing iron was slowly softening to my behind, but it was still somehow a long way off from feeling like a La-Z-Boy chair.

Wandering through the back streets of Arusha, we noticed a home that had many people coming and going from the entrance, so we decided to follow our noses and explore inside. It was a small house with a bedsheet draped over a piece of wire hanging across the door frame. Inside was a lady that everyone called 'Momma' who was cooking breakfast. Her home was her restaurant. We took a seat in two tiny plastic chairs that are normally reserved for children under five at a barbecue and asked for two plates of whatever she was cooking.

When we went to pay, Momma only charged us the same price as the locals. The meal totalled to mere cents in our currency. There was no up-charge for being a foreigner here. We had grown so accustomed to being charged extra in Africa, followed by something along the lines of, "You're white—you can afford it."

I am a believer in travelling to off-the-beaten-track countries for multiple reasons. The places that have not yet been exposed to mass tourism offer unique insights into daily life. With hop-on, hop-off double-decker tour buses and walking tours not yet established, local shop owners charge the actual going rate for products. There is no highly inflated tourist tax added on that is commonly found in heavily travelled countries. Now it is not that I haven't travelled to places like Rome or Paris, but I would prefer to sip a cup of chai in the back streets of Delhi than overpriced espressos in Italy and watch an empty desert sunset in Morocco over congested coastlines in Croatia. There is something to be said about roaming to more dirty, grungy, less-travelled countries. Sometimes it's not so much the sites, but the interactions you have with the local people that are more wholesome, as opposed to heavily touristic places.

On the days riding south of Arusha, we had the ever-majestic backdrop of Mount Kilimanjaro. Along with being the tallest mountain in Africa, this is also the highest single free-standing mountain above sea level in the world, standing at 5,895 metres. Mount Kilimanjaro was a sight to behold.

It was along these roads that we started to see more locals riding bicycles. Some were on old single-speed rusty bikes from the 1960s, while others were on a newer three-speed bike that became more frequent the further south we continued. We found out the newer, steel-framed, two-wheeled vessels were part of an aid project donation to a lot of eastern and southern Africa. The cyclists we came upon were carrying water jugs and boxes of food supplies from village to village. Some would tag behind us in a peloton, drafting for wind protection. We often found ourselves with two to three locals trailing behind us, hugging our rear tyres, pedalling flat-out, with their half-deflated tyres going *dadoof-dadoof*. When there were not any oncoming vehicles, they would speed up to ride next to us, smiling in conversation, and then would quickly slip back whenever a truck would come around a bend. There was so much joy in their faces.

It was at this stage through Tanzania that Mac's tyres started to collect any piece of glass or wire on the road. These were the same set of tyres that had seen her through Europe, and now halfway down Africa, they were starting to show a bit of wear. On one particular day, we had only cycled 65 kilometres and spent the rest of the hours picking everything from pieces of glass bottles to loose wire from Mac's rubber, carefully patching the inner tube after the surgery.

Most days on the bike, I chose to wear a long-sleeved khaki Columbia shirt. This shirt had been on my back more days than not for the last two years. It was starting to get thin where my backpack straps would sit over my shoulders, and now the blazing African sun was working its way through the material. While we resupplied on provisions in Singida, I found a young seamstress to sew a patch onto the shirt. She had done a superior job compared to my previous attempt to sew the holes with dental floss.

Up ahead, there was a section on the map that left Mac and I playing rock, paper, scissors on which direction to go. Our aim was to head southwest towards the border of Zambia. One way led us through two large open wildlife parks. Yes, you did read that right; open, meaning there were no fences. The road cut right through the reserve that was known for its large cats. Unlike domestic felines, 'cats' on this continent meant large, predatory lions. This excited Mac and me, yeah… well, for the lack of a better word—no! Otherwise, our Plan B would take us further southeast down to Dodoma, the capital of Tanzania, after which we would need to cut back westward, tacking on additional days to our ride.

By the afternoon, we reached the critical fork in the road. We turned right, towards the open parks, and left the ease of the pavement behind. Shortly after, we were greeted with deep ruts on a dirt road that eventually turned into soft sand tracks. Our progress diminished as enthusiasm leapt from my body. After an hour of pushing over miniature sandcastles, we decided that it would be faster to backtrack and route towards Dodoma, so we turned our bikes around and pushed through the sand for another hour until we reached the pavement again. Deep down I was grateful for those ruts and soft sand, otherwise we would have been cycling through big cat country.

After climbing the great Maasai Steppe and spending a couple of days in Iringa to recover, we reached the town of Mbeya, which meant we were only about 100 kilometres from the border of Tanzania and Zambia.

We left the following morning with a fair amount of traffic heading in our direction. Approaching a popular border crossing into Zambia meant increased traffic and a disappearing shoulder on the edge of the road. As if pedalling uphill was not taxing enough, we had the additional task of dodging countless cars and trucks.

The roads in Africa seem to orchestrate to a size ranking: a walker is the lowest on the food chain and needs to get out of the way first, followed closely by cyclists, then cars, small trucks, larger trucks, buses, and sitting at the top is a petrol or a logging truck. As a cyclist, if you meet any of these vehicles on the road, then you need to get out of their way swiftly.

On the way to the border, I had made it up the dreaded traffic-laden hill, only to look back and not see Mac behind me. My heart sank. I could see her in the distance on the side of the road, her bike on its side, and Mac bent over. I spun my bike around and pedalled towards the oncoming traffic.

A vehicle had clipped her rear pannier when they were passing Mac. Her bungee cord snapped, wrapping itself around her spokes and chain, which halted her bike instantly. Huddled on the side of the road with trucks and buses honking their horns as they flew past, we cut the bungee cord free from the chain, unwound it from the spokes, and got back on our bikes to once more tackle the hill ahead.

Throughout the rest of the day, I was still on high alert after Mac's vehicle incident. Descending a hill, I saw the brake lights of a bus up ahead. A second later, the bus took off in a plume of diesel fumes. We soon reached the area where the bus had been, which was now filled with a crowd of people gathered around what seemed to be a young male, no older than twenty. His body lay on the edge of the road, convulsing. Blood was spurting from his mouth. He wore the local tribal cloth around his waist and a machete tied to his hip.

Trying to quickly assess the situation, it appeared to us as though the boy may have stepped out to cross the road without looking and had been struck by the moving bus. The bus driver had not stopped to help and continued to drive, in an apparent hit-and-run situation. The group that had gathered around the boy seemed in utter shock and confusion. As a few onlookers rushed to the boy's aid, we were shaken by the sobering reality of the dangerous roads.

After encountering two terrifying situations for the day, we counted ourselves lucky to reach the final town before the Tanzania-Zambia border, called Vwawa. We called our day early, relaxing with a beer and reminiscing on both the good and bad of our last few eventful weeks riding through Tanzania.

James Beatty

CHAPTER 7

Surely, of all the wonders of the world, the horizon is the greatest.
—Freya Stark

Zambia & Zimbabwe

Crossing the border and waving our goodbyes to Tanzania, we could not help but think what a ride it had been through what the world recognizes as East Africa. Zambia lies at the crossroads of the Central, Southern, and Eastern regions of Africa. Surrounded by seven countries, the area used to make up what was previously known as Northern Rhodesia.

I was excited to be heading further south toward our goal. Albeit slowly, we were getting there. Our bikes were holding up well, Mac had not had a flat tyre in a handful of days. I could now shift cogs after replacing the broken cable in Nairobi and, hey, would you believe it, even my seat was slowly getting softer.

If I am being honest, when someone would mention the word Africa, what I had envisioned was East Africa, full of bright colours, wild animals, some war and conflict, disorganised traffic, and friendly faces, but also people who had hardly ever laid eyes on a white person before. Rough around the edges, these lands had their scars and wounds, whether that is from recent conflicts or from their colonial pasts.

We were thrilled to be in Zambia, and looking at our map while exchanging the last of our Tanzanian shillings, we could see that we were getting much lower on the map of the continent. Passing through each country, we observed certain changes in infrastructure among the roads, buildings, and street layouts. Each country had its own focus and issues they were working on.

The road conditions in the north of Zambia were horrendous, to say the least. Heading south along the Tanzam Highway, we were greeted by the worst road surfaces that we had come upon on this adventure so far. Let me just say that seeing the words 'Great' or 'Highway' on a road sign did not live up to any thought that it might have been a well-laid road.

This highway, in particular, was the worst damn road we had ridden on in the entirety of Africa so far. What had passed as the road was no more than a mix between old, compacted dirt and asphalt that had been laid twenty years ago, with potholes so deep that you actually considered the possibility that a comet had fallen from the sky and recently struck the earth.

There was only one patch of the road, measuring about a truck's width, that had been laid with asphalt. The rest was just sand and mud. We would be cycling along on the asphalt until two trucks would overtake us, fighting for which of them would keep driving on the paved, meteor-stricken runway, while the other unlucky contender would have no choice but to swerve into the sand.

As for us, since we were much lower in the vehicle food chain, we were given no option but to dive off the road as the trucks would sound their horns telling us to get out of their way, otherwise, we would be food for the birds and wild animals. After the repetitive highway musical chairs, we would dust ourselves off, stand amongst the shrubs and pull the finger at the truck driver, only to get the same treatment from every other passing truck.

On that first afternoon in Zambia, we stopped in a small town called Kalungu. We were in search of a SIM card so we could contact our families and let them know we had crossed the border safely. The village was compact, a one-street kind of town. There were two stores selling drinks and biscuits, another shop nearby cut hair, and everything else looked like it had been closed and boarded up for years.

Some locals gathered out under the shade of one of the stores, drinking a homemade brew that smelled something like a donkey had drunk a bottle of vodka and you had been there to bottle his urine first thing the following morning. It seemed to have its desired effect, though.

Across from that riveting scene was a school that had a fresh coat of bright blue paint on it and some new roofing iron. At the field of the school stood a young enterprising male who had set up a kiosk selling SIM cards, and not just any SIM cards, these were pre-registered ones. We went up and asked him for two. He did not need our documents, nor our names. We merely handed him some cash, and he gave us the SIM cards. It would not be until we reached Lusaka that we found out that our names needed to be registered to the SIM cards in order to top them up with money and keep using them. I'm not sure where our friendly, business-savvy teenager had gotten these bootleg versions, but it saved us a lot of time and hassle.

During the exchange of the SIM cards, one local who was sitting under the shade drinking the local brew came over to meet the two white foreigners on bicycles. He told us there was a camp down the road where we could inquire about spending the night.

We followed his directions down a sandy track, past some thatched and earthed homes, and reached the Kings Highway Campground. It was a peaceful sanctuary, tucked about two kilometres away from town, surrounded by a vast array of trees and gardens that lie around a dozen bungalows. After setting up our tent, we got talking to the couple that ran the camp. We found out there are a few of these Kings Highway rest camps scattered throughout Southern Africa, set up by a religious group that moves around in remote areas to create jobs and help build schools and other dwellings. They build a rest camp for any passing tourists and then use that money to help fund the other projects they have in the area. Although I am not the religious sort, on the surface, this seemed to be a group that was helping on the local grassroots level.

Over the next few days, we rode past clusters of four or five mud brick homes at a time, each with thatched roofs and neatly swept dirt yards, with kids selling some mangos freshly plucked from the trees out front. It was incredible to see some villages that looked as if time had stood still since the days of Livingstone and Stanley. Locals would wave our way, saying hello as we rolled by.

We did not see stressed and tired-looking faces as is familiar in our Western money-fed countries. Instead, we saw a very relaxed pace of life. The people grew what they ate, had a handful of cows and goats, and bartered their harvests and goods with surrounding families. They did not spend their entire day working. The locals tended to the animals in the mornings, gathered the water needed for the day from the local well, and the kids would be playing or out with the mothers in the fields collecting food and wood for the fires. There seemed to be a balance of harmony going on. Time had really stood still, and it was unforgettable to witness.

My fascination for visiting remote villages around the world has grown over this past decade of travelling. I wanted to see with my own eyes distant places that have not yet been modernised by the Western world.

Before coming to Africa, while travelling through Central Asia, one night stands out in my mind while I was visiting villages deep in the Wakhan Corridor on the border of Afghanistan. Just days before the US troops had pulled out of Afghanistan, there were people fleeing into Tajikistan through this narrow stretch of land. A local family had taken me in for the night. While we sat around the fire waiting for the meat stew to cook, I could not help but notice a young boy had slipped through the door and looked to be getting help with his schoolwork. The oldest daughter of the family was one of the few teachers in the valley who would spend her spare time in the evenings helping any of the local children. While talking with her, I asked how much she earned. She replied with $150 a year. Yeah, I know what you're thinking. I thought the same thing—*that can't be right... must have been the language barrier.* So I translated the question into Tajik. Her response was the same. She earned $150 a year for working full time as a teacher and gave up her evenings free of charge to help the young children.

Now, in reading that story, it affects you differently if you have not seen and experienced it with your own eyes. That is why I love travelling to some of the far-flung places that still exist in our world. When I proceeded to ask if there was any depression or anxiety amongst the people in this small village, the lady's face showed a puzzled expression. Her response was, "No, we don't have that here."

Life was simple and their minds were not flooded with the thoughts of, *do I have enough? Am I enough? Do I look a certain way?* They lived a life that rotated around the essentials.

As humans, what we need to survive is quite basic: food, water, and air. You can throw shelter, heat, love, and purpose into the mix as well, but those are just add-ons. Yet we find ourselves piling more and more layers of stress onto our lives. From what I've witnessed, a lot of these people, whom the Western world would deem 'severely poor,' are much happier and richer on a deeper level than any of us in our Western countries. During my travels through the Wakhan Corridor, I began to understand the key to true happiness lies in simplicity.

The rainy monsoon season in Africa was setting in. For the last week, we could see clouds forming and slowly growing darker each afternoon. We woke up and left Matumbo early, noticing that the first rain of the season looked to be brewing. The sky was dark with thunderous purple and grey clouds sitting on the horizon. We rode for as long as we could until the clouds were right over the top of us.

With thunder and lightning above, I quickly waved down a small white Japanese-style Ute carrying baskets of coal and asked the driver if we could get a hitch to the nearest town. We threw our bikes on top of the tightly packed coal baskets and tucked ourselves next to the cab to try to seek a little shelter just as the clouds bellowed above. We pulled our ponchos over top of us and tried to not get completely drenched. As the rain and thunder were falling, the roads soon became awash with turbulent amounts of water and mud. We held on, white-knuckled, as we could not see what was coming up ahead, ears ringing with thunder and the deafening crack of lightning directly overhead adding to my growing list of unforgettable occurrences along this African adventure.

Later in the day, we made it to Mpika. The rain had stopped, and our bodies were slowly drying out. We rode up to a petrol station and were amazed at the sight; it was small but reminded us of a Western-style station selling meat pies and sausage rolls. We stood facing the pie rack for what must have been five minutes, deciding which steaming hot pie we would eat. Some hot, tasty goodness on a cold, wet day was a treat.

Looking at our damp and tattered map, I found a guesthouse that was known by other overlanders. We cycled down the road until we found Bayamas Lodge. It was owned by a German expat who had stayed in Zambia after working in the nearby mines for years. The lodge had a campground, restaurant, bar, an outdoor area with an array of tables and chairs, a pool table, and about six rooms, all catering towards overlanders. We got talking with the expat owner and he told us we were some of his only customers for the year. We spent the evening warming up and drying our clothes, playing pool, and sipping on some of Zambia's finest beers.

It was December 22, and by the time we rode into the capital night had already fallen. With our headlights blinking and our hi-vis vests on, we navigated through the busy intersections of Lusaka to find a hostel. Entering a busy capital for the first time is normally nerve-racking enough, let alone attempting it in the dark.

It was a vast contrast from where we had been to where we were now. In the previous weeks, we had either camped or stayed in little run-down rooms that were part of a brothel system that each roadside town seemed to be running, with the passing truck drivers being their main clientele. Apart from the missionary camp in the north of the country and the German in Mpika, we had not seen any mzungus that were travelling around.

I have lost track of how many hostels I have visited while travelling these past ten years. I have worked in them, volunteered, partied, and just passed on through. In the common room of a hostel, I have made some of my greatest friends. This hostel in Lusaka was our first on the African journey that resembled one that you would find in Latin America or Southeast Asia. I looked around to see the familiar setup: a reception, maps hanging on the walls, tattered books stacked on the bookshelf, and a communal kitchen where dishes lay piled up like Tetris. A large common area with chairs and tables and countless poorly lit rooms filled with bunk beds resembled an army barracks. It felt like home!

With the holiday only a few days away, Mac and I decided we would spend Christmas in Lusaka. It would be enjoyable to unwind and spend a few nights in one place, which we had not done since Nairobi.

In the following days, we met other travellers wandering around parts of this incredible continent. There was a guy who had purchased a cheap second-hand Suzuki motorbike, riding it around the southern part of Africa. We also met a girl who had been volunteering for a water project in the neighbouring country of Malawi, and a trio in a 4x4 who wanted to drive the exact route that Mac and I had just come from. The three had started in Cape Town two weeks ago and were hoping to reach Cairo in their Toyota Land Cruiser. We hit it off with all the vagabonds that were staying in the hostel, and come Christmas Eve, partied and danced to the live music as if we were back in one of our own countries.

Once Christmas had passed, it was time to get back on our bikes. Our next stop was somewhere that had been high on my list of places to visit for some time: Livingstone. I had read books about the explorer David Livingstone, whom the town was named after, and his adventures through Africa.

One of the earliest Europeans recorded to have visited this area was a Portuguese explorer named Francisco de Lacerda at the end of the 18th century. After his travels here, other explorers made their way over during the 19th century, one of which, most famously known, was David Livingstone. He happened to be the first European to set eyes on the magnificent waterfalls on the Zambezi River in 1855, naming them Victoria Falls, after the Queen of England. I had heard that there was a museum down in the town of Livingstone that was filled with David's old journals and letters, as well as a lot of his old belongings, like a first aid kit and some of his clothing. I was looking forward to getting to see some of these after reading so much about the explorer.

We roamed around Livingstone, exploring the majestic Victoria Falls and the local museum, as well as going to visit one of the old traditional colonial resorts that sits on the shores of the river. We crossed the bridge over the Zambezi River and ventured into Zimbabwe, but after closer examination of the map, saw that the most direct route toward the upcoming Elephant Highway was the border connecting Zambia to Botswana. So, after a brief visit to Zimbabwe, we returned across the bridge and reentered Zambia.

We spent a morning navigating around the public hospital in Livingstone, trying to find a small building where we were told we could have a Covid test taken. Each land crossing that we had gone through in Africa required a negative test to be shown at the border.

After we finally found where the tests were taken, we were asked, "Do you have your payment receipt?"

"No," I replied, "no one had told us that we needed to pay elsewhere for the test."

"Yes sir, you need to go to the main entrance of the hospital, where you will see a small building on your left. You must pay there first before receiving your test."

So off we rode back through the hospital complex. It took twenty minutes to find the right building through the maze of old concrete and brick hospital blocks, and now we were sent back to the start of the maze. I could not find the elusive sign saying 'Pay Here' for the Covid tests. They had neglected to put one up.

We waited until someone finally had finished their lunch break and came back into the office only to inform us, "Sorry sir, we only accept cash."

I was fuming!

Back on the bikes, we rode to the nearest bank that had a working ATM. By this stage, I must add I was getting pretty fed up, but Mac soon refreshed my memory that we were still in Africa. Livingstone is fairly developed in terms of Western comforts such as banks, grocery stores, and cafes, but in the end, we were still in Africa. Waiting in a queue of people for the bank, all I could do was smile and grit my teeth.

With our pockets stuffed full of cash, we headed back to the small office, paid the lady, got our receipt, and rode on to the building at the back of the hospital complex for our tests. In a quick fifteen minutes later, we had our nostrils poked and prodded with a cotton ear bud and we were on our way. This entire roundabout episode took us well over three hours.

The next morning, we packed up our gear and headed to yet another building, this one on the opposite side of town to collect our results. We stood and waited with a group of locals and two other foreigners, an older German couple overlanding in their 4x4 through Southern Africa.

After four hours of waiting, a nurse finally came out and told the group that in the batch of thirty people, two tests came back positive. The only problem was that they did not know which ones were the positives, so proceeded to retest them all again, which now reported 28 positive tests. She said that a doctor would come out soon to explain more.

It sounded like while they were trying to decipher the positive test, they had actually cross-contaminated nearly the whole batch. The doctor soon appeared, looking somewhat sheepish, and told everyone, "You all tested positive for Covid-19, please go immediately to your homes, isolate for two weeks, and then come back and we will test you all again."

And just like that, we had wasted $120 and a whole day, only to be gently smacked in the face to show us, hey you're still in Africa, don't think it's over yet.

By the time we got back on our bikes, it was early afternoon. We decided to book one more night at our guesthouse, then in the morning we would just ride to the border and try our luck crossing without a test.

The following morning, as we made our way toward the border, we were passed on the road by the German couple in their 4x4. As we stopped and chatted, they told us they had found a private lab in town yesterday afternoon and got a new Covid test, which came back negative. It was official, the hospital's testing facility had botched the results.

An hour later, we were in the Botswana

immigration office, hoping there was some way we could take a Covid test at the border and not have to ride all the way back to Livingstone. We explained to an officer that we did not realise the border did not offer Covid tests and had biked all this way. The officer got his manager, who after making us wait for him, told us to wait some more.

At that instant, I turned my head and noticed some truck drivers in the distance getting their tests taken. I said to the officer, "How is it that the lorry drivers are getting tests done here?"

And just like that, with no more questions asked, we got our noses prodded with a Q-tip. We could not help but to shake our heads at the ongoing bureaucracy of the current pandemic that was unfolding around the globe. Thirty minutes later, we were handed our negative results and were on our way into Botswana.

CHAPTER 8

Wilderness. The word itself is magic.
—Edward Abbey

Botswana

Botswana is home to the world's largest population of elephants. There are roughly 130,000 of these almost mythical, larger-than-life African creatures still roaming around. What makes this place such a hub for the elephants is that in the north of Botswana, where four countries verge together—Namibia, Zambia, Zimbabwe, and Botswana—it has been the migratory pathway for these spectacular mammals on their own tour of Southern Africa for hundreds of years. And here we found ourselves on what is known as The Elephant Highway.

The clouds grew dark, and soon the sky was filled with aggression. A bolt of lightning fired from the heavens up above and the sound of thunder rumbled as I was trying to count the seconds to calculate how far away it was. The purple sky had now turned into ebony as we cycled into the ferocious beast ahead. We had finally caught up to the rainy season.

We set up the tent and rolled inside, just as the thunder and rain started to fall. We celebrated making it into our eighth country on this trip with some lunch and a pleasant afternoon nap while listening to the raindrops tap on the tent. There are not too many things more relaxing in life than lying inside a tent and listening to the rain fall outside. *As long as your tent is waterproof and isn't leaking like a sieve, that is.*

That evening, we spoke with a South African family that was on an overlanding trip through Namibia and Botswana in two 4x4 Toyota Land Cruisers. Both were decked out with pop-top tents, awnings, tables, chairs, hammocks, and a portable fire pit. You name it, I'm pretty damn sure they had it packed away in those vehicles. We spent that evening scanning over the map and jotting down their recommendations on where to stop on our way down to the Cape.

In the morning, we set off on the road known as the Elephant Highway. We were no more than five kilometres from the previous night's campground when we came across our first herd of elephants standing on the edge of the road. Now coming from New Zealand, nothing could quite prepare me to see these animals up close in the wild. Their sheer size was breathtaking. As we rolled up along the pavement towards where they were feeding, the elephants quickly scared off, stomping the earth as they headed back into the bush. It was sensational to see them out in nature roaming wild and freely under their own will. But nothing could have prepared me for what was about to happen thirty minutes later.

Without warning, a male elephant blew out of the bushes to my left as we were humming along on a beautiful straight section of road. It was at this second that I abruptly recalled advice from the South African father from the previous night. "Whatever you do, steer clear of a male bull elephant in heat!" He followed the warning with a few different signs of what to look for if we found ourselves in the situation.

And, well, at the moment I saw the male elephant darting from the bushes, there was one of those clear signs he had mentioned. "His old fella will almost be dragging on the ground," the father had blurted. And if we did find ourselves a horny male elephant, "Get the hell out of his damn way!" the father had shouted, in a thick Afrikaans accent.

A nightmarish fraction of a second had passed since the elephant had stormed out from the trees and I had noticed his you-know-what. I quickly slammed on the brakes and turned the bike around, only to see that the immense beast was charging straight at me, making disturbing noises and flapping his ears. It was the sort of scene that makes you sit back while watching the Discovery Channel and think, *wow how neat,* only I did not have the time to think back in case the father had mentioned anything else if we got this far into an encounter.

Survival instinct kicked in, and I jumped on my pedal immediately to steer my bike in the direction away from this gigantic thunderous grey mass. The moment I slammed down on my pedal, I felt the chain spin into what I could only describe as fresh air. I heard a horrifying *ping…* the damn thing had just snapped! I turned back to see the elephant charging and closing the gap.

Then, suddenly, he came to a halt!

In a split second, I had gone from being a mere moment away from shitting in my undies, to now looking straight into the elephant's eyes. Time stopped at that instant. I followed his long eyelashes blinking as he examined me up and down. I noticed the deep creases on his trunk and nails growing out of his massive feet. It was as close to an out-of-body experience as I have ever had.

And then, as quick as the mock charge had happened, he took off back into the bushes across the road. As I stood there dripping in sweat and panting, Mac rode up, after having witnessed the whole thing from about twenty-five metres back when the elephant had burst out of the trees.

Senses regained, I then recalled the father saying, "the elephant will do a false charge, then they will decide what you are, and if they are going to attack or not."

It must have been my lucky day, I thought to myself. With a few more points gained on the great wheel of karma, I was still shaking, similar to when you've climbed too high up on a diving board, peer over the edge toward the pool and decide you want down that second. I quickly fixed my broken chain link and got back on our way, not feeling the need to hang around in case my new friend came back.

The weather now was predictable, the rainy season was among us. We dodged the sudden storms whenever we could, avoiding bursts of heavy monsoon rain that fell by hiding under our ponchos or a structure if it was nearby. By the time it reached 4 p.m. the dark clouds had closed in around us and the wind was blowing strong.

A man and his son pulled up in their Ute next to me and yelled out through the half-rolled-down window, "Hop on in!"

There wasn't any introduction—no hello, how are you, would you like a ride? So, I just replied with, "No, we're alright thanks." Reluctantly, the man drove away, and I was left confused by the entire situation.

The wind was howling at this stage and making our progress stupidly slow. We still had twenty-eight kilometres to go until we would reach our destination for the night, a gas station up ahead. At our pace, it would take us three more hours.

In Botswana, we had been warned not to camp out in the open wilderness because of so many lions being around. People had said to look for a structure—a fence, antenna tower, even a gas station or a building if we could find one.

We were told, "The cats won't bother you if you camp near something that is man-made and foreign to them."

After finally deciding to give up cycling into the permanent hair-splitting wind, I flagged down the next vehicle that drove past us, and the driver turned out to be a wildlife worker. She worriedly informed us that we should not be out on the road at this time and to quickly hop in. It was only 4:30 p.m. but because it was much darker thanks to the rainy season, the lions had started to come out to hunt much earlier. For someone who had grown up on a small island where the only predators were an odd mouse or possum, I had never had to worry about anything large enough that could attack a human. This was quite the change.

We piled the bikes in the back of the pick-up truck, and she dropped us off at the gas station in Pandamatenga. At the fuel stations in Botswana, we noticed that security guards were always on duty at night to watch the pumps.

We asked the ladies in the small convenience store if we could camp the night, and they replied, "Sure thing, but you have to make sure the security guard doesn't mind."

We asked the guard if it was alright, and after he took my bike on a small ride around the petrol pumps, he gave us the approval to camp in the area he was patrolling. And so, after a rather eventful day, we were sitting back to some cold baked beans out of a tin, our tent pitched on the ground next to a petrol pump, and we even had a private security guard keeping an eye out for the night.

In the night I was suddenly awoken by heavy rain pelting our tent. Now what I had said a few pages back, about there not being many things that beat falling asleep in a tent while it's raining... well something that does beat that, is waking up in the middle of the night to the tent flooded!

It had rained so much in such a short time that

we found ourselves in a mini Noah's Ark. There were ten centimetres of water all around us, our sleep pads floating in a newly formed lake, and all our gear was completely soaked.

We quickly grabbed our belongings and threw them over to the sheltered overhang of the store. We dismantled the tent and set it up next to our gear under the overhang. The funniest thing about that entire ordeal was that our new security friend sat on his wooden stall under the shelter the entire time, watching us and our ark taking on water and having to move everything. He clearly enjoyed the entertainment.

Each day of riding in Botswana we were getting further and further away from the mud huts of East Africa and were now seeing more developed townships with paved roads, footpaths, and streetlights, but noticed they were struggling with the same things that we see in our own Western countries. There were now security guards at any supermarket that we stopped at. Outside of liquor stores were the lingering village drunks.

The West had made it over to this part of Africa, and it was apparent. People had come from their land to live closer to the townships so that they could work and get paid in paper currency. Most had cheap smartphones that they stuffed into their pockets or held inches from their faces. That technology occupied a lot of the youths that we passed. There was also crime, drunkenness, and poverty—specifically the kind of poverty that I like to call, 'poverty of the mind.' When caught in the act of thinking you need more, always chasing the carrot dangling out in front, you never quite have enough of what you want, all the while tricking yourself into thinking it is what you need.

Some of the richest people I have met across the globe have very few possessions. They hardly make any money, but they have everything they could ever need and in this true beauty, they have no desire for more. This is similar to the Zen Buddhist approach of 'when you are finally there, it will be just like here.' Let go of material desires and you will be free.

Botswana was the type of riding we had both dreamt of. The roads were flat, traffic was lean, and a tailwind pushed us along most days, until it was time to stop and seek shelter, and allow the afternoon downpour to pass us by. As we whizzed by on our bikes, we saw elephants, giraffes, and zebras all along the edge of the road grazing.

Cycling was one of those activities that allowed our conscious 'thinking mind' to shut down for a little while. To some, they consider this a meditative state. Others call it a 'flow state.' Time seemed to stand still but yet flew by, all within the same instance, similar to moments while hiking in the mountains or deserts where all small, trivial thoughts that seem to fill the brain on a daily basis just drop away and you are left just in motion. The body is on autopilot mode and the mind shuts off, taking a break. It is the closest feeling to what I could only imagine of being a soaring bird, catching drafts of wind and gliding from one updraft to another. Other than having to dodge aroused male elephants or looking around for lions in nearby bushes or up trees, I would slip away into the sky, soaring as free as a bird with my wings outstretched.

We had stopped under a tree one mid-morning to have some lunch when in the distance I spotted two white dots on bicycles coming in our direction.

I announced the news to Mac. "It looks like there are two mzungus up ahead."

We both stood and waved at what felt like two aliens in this distant, remote land, who happened to be performing the exact same act that we were doing. Soon enough we met David and Caroline, an English and French couple, who were cycling around the world in hopes of obtaining the Guinness World Record for the fastest married couple to ride around the globe. We talked about their ride through Africa that they had just started from Cape Town not so long ago. We gathered some information from them on road conditions and areas where we could resupply and collect water. Our conversation was brief; they had to get back on their saddles to keep on their daily target. We kept in touch with them over the coming months and later found out that they did complete their goal and now hold the title of the 'fastest bicycle circumnavigation by a married couple.'

Our mileage throughout Botswana was dictated by the shops, houses, structures, or towers we could find on our map to camp at the day's end. As we worked our way over to the west of Botswana, we found ourselves in big game territory. With signs on the main road reading the instructions 'Game Hunting: turn right in 250 metres' I thought to myself, *so this is where trophy hunters travel from around the world to satisfy their urge to kill something big.*

A lot of campgrounds had unexpectedly had to close due to the effects of Covid and the lack of tourism, so we were not entirely certain if our destination was open until we arrived. We approached a camp that was a family's house, seeing a sign that said they were open. Out the back, they had created a campground. We met the owner and her daughter and chatted with them. I asked if there were many lions in the area. The mother confirmed with, "Oi yeah! Those buggers get through our fences and kill some of our cattle from time to time."

Fantastic, I thought, *lovely to hear that the fences don't keep the lions out and if they really want in, then they'll easily come on through!* Thanks to the person earlier in Botswana who suggested camping next to fences and that we would be just fine.

We reached the town of Ghanzi, which sits in the middle of the Kalahari Desert. We rode around trying to find somewhere to stay for the night, but everything was out of our budget. We stopped at a supermarket to grab a meat pie and a sausage roll when an old Boer farmer walked over and asked us where we were going to stay for the night. He told us about a place right on the outskirts of town that had burnt down. The new owners were rebuilding the rooms and would surely give us a low rate. We followed his suggestion and found accommodation for the night.

At about two in the morning, I woke to a rumble in my stomach—the sort that when woken, you don't wait around for a second warning. I quickly dashed to the toilet, emptying the contents of the meat pie that I had scoffed down in the afternoon, along with the warmed-up chicken that we had for dinner, found on the market's sale rack.

When the sun rose in the morning, my butt felt like it had lava pouring out. It was safe to say I wasn't that keen for a big day in the saddle. This was meant to be our last day in Botswana.

I had heard quite a bit about Namibia from

travellers I had met around the world in the last decade, excited by the stories that were filled with amazingly different landscapes and a coastline I was itching to see after so many landlocked months without being by the sea.

The remaining mileage in Botswana took us no time, and we pulled up to the immigration building before midday. We had heard from another traveller that this was a simple and seamless crossing from Botswana into Namibia. He reported that the immigration building had a Covid test machine, and it would take only thirty minutes to get our test results and then continue on through to the Namibia border post.

We walked into the building, filled out the leaving form, and handed it to the officer. He then asked to see our Covid test results.

We responded with, "We'll just take the test here with your machine."

After which the officer said, "Ahhh, our machine broke two days ago."

I couldn't believe what we were hearing. We were so close to Namibia, standing at the border, yet now unable to get a test taken.

I searched for any hope, asking, "Well, when will it be fixed?"

The officer responded, "We don't know, it could be a day, could be a month."

Ahhhhh Africa, we had heard the saying 'T.A.B' during our time throughout the continent. That's. Africa. Baby. It was beyond true, the simplest of things can sometimes be made so difficult here in Africa.

The officer said, "You will need to go to Ghanzi, there is a lab there where you can take a test."

Ghanzi? Ghanzi was 200 kilometres back! *He made it sound like it was just down the damn road.*

The more we talked to the officer, and with Africa being well, Africa, you can sometimes give a little donation with a smile and a wink, and they look the other way. This did actually work on the Botswana side, but the officer said, "I will let you go across to the Namibian immigration building and you can ask if they will let you through without a test." In which they did not, so we were back after a mere minute in Namibia.

The officer volunteered for us to leave our bikes at his house, which was nearby. So, we rolled our bikes across the road, locked them up in the backyard, walked out to the roadside, and stuck out our thumbs, headed back to Ghanzi.

I am fond of hitchhiking. I've spent years hitchhiking around Europe, Canada, the USA, and Australia. It was the way I knew how to get around on the cheap and a genuine way to see the kindness of a country and its people.

Our first ride came from a car filled with locals that we soon discovered were drunk. It was a Saturday afternoon, and they were off to a nearby village to get more of the cheap booze that had gotten into their current state. They dropped us near a bus stop on the outskirts of the village. Next, we waved down a nice-looking SUV that was passing by. They were Chinese workers who were employed in the nearby mines in Namibia and Botswana.

They had just come from Namibia and were driving across Botswana in the day to get to their camp at the mine site. With what took us over a day of riding, we were now staring out of the window, flying on the open road at 180 kilometres per hour. In what felt like I had just blinked, the three miners were dropping us off at a major intersection, handing us bottled water and waving goodbye as they sped off. We were now just a stone's throw to Ghanzi. Those 200 kilometres had vanished in no time.

The last ride came from a mechanic with a pick-up truck. We jumped in the back with old tyres, wrenches, and the wind blowing through our hair. This was a delightful change to the speedy ride we had just had in the SUV that left us both feeling somewhat motion sick. After months of slow travel on our bikes, our eyes and minds were taking some adjusting to the speeds that a motor vehicle can travel at.

The mechanic dropped us off in the heart of Ghanzi and we found ourselves back where we had been just days before. This time, on a mission. It was late Saturday afternoon; businesses would be closing shortly and would not be reopening until Monday morning. The hospital and clinics were already closed.

We got the name of a private clinic from a helpful hotel clerk. We wandered to the office only to find it closed, but we rang the number posted on the door in the hopes we would not have to wait for Monday. An older man answered and said he was just out walking but would swing by the clinic shortly to chat with us.

Once he arrived, we explained that we required a PCR test. He told us that they did not get tested here in Ghanzi. The hospital and other clinics would take the swabs and then put the test tubes on a bus to Maun, the town where we had taken a rest day last week. But all of that could take 48 hours until the results were sent back to his office. He was a lovely old man from Malawi, and after telling him we were cycling the African continent, he said, "Let me see if I can make some calls and pull some strings."

After putting the phone down, he told us to

come back in the morning and would take our nasal swabs then. From there, he would pay a bus driver to drop our tests off in Maun, after which his friend, who worked at the testing laboratory, would run our swabs first thing Monday and we should have our results emailed to us by lunchtime that same day.

Feeling relieved, we thanked the old man and headed to the supermarket to get some food for dinner, this time staying clear of the meat pies and warmed-up chicken. What a day it had been—from waking up early, packing away our camp, riding 100 kilometres, sorting out immigration, and taking a step into Namibia, to then hitching the three rides back to town and walking around to sort out the damn Covid tests. We were drained.

As the sun rose the next day, we were out on the side of the road, thumbing a ride into town to get our noses swabbed at the clinic. We had to pay $90 each. These Covid tests were not cheap and would be some of the most expensive tests that we had taken over the last two years of this entire pandemic.

It puzzled me that countries like New Zealand and the USA were charging $250 for a PCR Test and taking up to 48 hours to get the results back from the lab. In contrast, in Turkey, it costs $12 for the same test, and you get the results back in six hours. Absolutely astonishing!

Once we had our nasal cavities poked and prodded, we then grabbed some provisions and headed back to the roadside to hitch a ride back to our bikes on the border. We got a ride most of the way from one vehicle and then jumped in with a lorry driver for the last few kilometres to the Botswana-Namibia border. After collecting our bikes, we cycled back along the road to a newly built truck stop just 500 metres back along the pavement.

Making friends with the workers at the truck stop, they all took turns riding our bikes around the petrol pumps, weaving in and out like slalom racers. We asked their manager if we could camp there for the night. It was a Western-style truck stop, with a large fuel pump area, a parking lot for trucks to pull up and sleep overnight, a large covered-in tuck shop serving hot food and cold drinks, and a nice and clean toilet and shower block. Not an awful place to spend an afternoon and night. By the evening, the truck drivers all sat around drinking and asking about our stories. Most of them had driven the same route that we had taken through Zambia and Botswana and knew all the local villages that we had stopped in.

The next morning came, we packed up and waited for the email from the lab to come in. Our old Malawi doctor was right, and we received our results around noon. We jumped on our bikes and rode back to the immigration building. By this stage, everyone there knew of our story. We were the two white people riding on bicycles for the past few days in this tiny settlement next to the border.

Within two minutes, we had our passports stamped out of Botswana and they all wished us luck on finishing our ride to Cape Town. We rode to the Namibia border station, filled in the forms, and handed over our Covid test results. And with a clink of the immigration stamp in our passports, we were now in Namibia, our second to last country on this journey.

James Beatty

CHAPTER 9

If we have never been amazed by the very fact that we exist, we are squandering the greatest fact of all.
—Will Durant

Namibia

The country and the people that had lived here for many centuries found themselves under German rule back in 1884, known as German South West Africa. But after World War I, the Germans were defeated by the South African British and Dutch and the land soon came under South African rule in a bit of a tug-of-war between the Germans, the British, and the Dutch of South Africa. In 1990, Namibia finally gained their own independence. From our first instance, Namibia felt like a mix of cultures.

Only ten percent of the roads throughout the country are paved and when you are not on these roads, you are either riding on jutted dirt paths or just plain sand. The road we were travelling was paved in the north of the country, although they had neglected a shoulder for any potential cyclists. It got rather grim in some areas, with the roads being as narrow as a minuscule country road in rural New Zealand. The drivers' mindset seemed similar to those back home. They did not feel the need to give a cyclist any space, brushing inches past our elbows and panniers. Namibian drivers would prove to be the worst that we had come across on our whole trip down the continent, with the count of near-misses far exceeding any other country.

We had been told about a village called Seeis and an old gentleman who ran a small convenience store out of a decommissioned train carriage that sat on the tracks that nature had now started to take back over.

His name was Bennie. We arrived just as he was closing for the day, and he pulled out three icy-cold beers from his cooler near the counter and we started chatting. He loved hearing where we had been and was stacked with knowledge about the country and towns where we would be going in the coming weeks. While enjoying the dew-dripping can of beer in my hand and talking, I could see a rather burly looking storm closing in on the horizon. As we quickly pulled out the tent to set it up next to the train carriage, the storm was suddenly on top of us. The wind howled as it hit, knocking over a nearby ice cream sign. Our tent poles folded onto themselves, and the thin nylon walls nearly ripped in two from the force of the wind.

Bennie yelled to head over to his house, which was close by in a neighbouring paddock. We grabbed everything and ran, as the wind and rain were pelting down like sheets of carpenter's nails being thrown at us.

Moments later, standing there, dripping wet in their front walkway, Bennie and his wife offered for us to stay in their spare room and cook us a nice hot meal. We could not turn down an offer like that and soon we were sitting up sipping another beer, freshly bathed, and talking about the history of the country with this lovely older couple.

Moments like these are what I truly love about travelling. It's the generosity of complete strangers that open up their homes, all within only a short amount of time spent with them, when you feel there might still be a brief glimmer of hope for the world and society.

By the morning, the storm had passed. After a cup of coffee, we said goodbye to Bennie and his wife and rode on towards the capital of Windhoek. The roads wrapped around the mountain contours and eventually opened up to the country's capital.

Before Windhoek was a city, it was a hot spring that was only known by the local indigenous people who resided in the area. In 1840, Jonker Afrikaner, a political captain for the Oorlam People, ventured up with his followers, leaving behind South Africa for another land and settling upon the hot spring. Jonker and his people built a church for their Christian congregation and from there it grew into a town and eventually the city that we found ourselves riding into.

Windhoek is not overly large or busy by Western standards, but we were far away from the land that your mind takes you to when someone mentions the word Africa. With coffee shops on most street corners, malls, and restaurants, we had well and truly left the mud hut villages behind and were now in the modern and ever-developing Southern Africa.

After three days of eating Western food and wandering around the capital, we headed out towards Solitaire, left behind the paved roads, and took to the 4x4 routes that were either sand, clay or rock.

We approached a car that had gotten stuck while crossing a river. We tried to help, but our efforts were essentially useless, apart from a little morale which was all we could add to the driver's misfortune.

Further up at another river crossing, we saw a semi-truck that was stuck smack bang in the middle of the river. Now, coming up to a sight like this, you almost had to double-take at the situation. A semi-truck. In the middle of a river. Surrounded by soft sand.

Looking at the scene, I could not help but laugh to myself. *How the heck did he find himself here?* I thought. We spoke to the hapless driver to see if he was okay and had plenty of food and water because he looked like he might be waiting there awhile. I have a feeling he was trying to bypass authorities by smuggling the semi-truck through from Angola along the coast. We had heard of a few occurrences where this sort of mischief happened on these back roads.

We finally reached Solitaire, a small, dust-blown town of one gas pump, one bakery, and a general store, that had coined its name from a farmer's wife. Willem Christoffel van Coller bought 33,000 hectares of land to farm a few sheep. His wife, Elise Sophia van Coller, gave the area its name, Solitaire, meaning a single set diamond. Combined with this remote solitude, you get a name that means a one-of-a-kind, solitary place.

Whether it is at the pyramids in Egypt, the middle of the deserts in Kenya, or the lush wetlands of Botswana—some of the purest sunsets are to be witnessed here in Africa. As that gigantic bulge of burning gas started to lower itself towards the horizon, we were gifted an exquisite sunset on Mac's birthday. We celebrated surrounded by mountains in the middle of the ever-changing landscape. With wildebeest and oryx roaming in the distance, there was a gorgeous deep orange glow from the dipping sun, and no other sign of human life as far as we could see.

Mac had treated herself to buying a cotton dress while we were in Windhoek. After months of wearing bike shorts and long sleeves to cover up from the harsh sun, she had been dreaming of wearing a dress again. That night, she looked beyond stunning.

We spend most of our time on adventures, cycling, climbing, and hiking around the world. In total, we have spent more nights in a tent sleeping on the earth's floor than we have on a mattress in a room over the last six years. Even though we have carried and worn the same clothes with us for years, just seeing her in a fresh cotton dress set off the same butterflies in my stomach as I had when I first met her in Costa Rica.

We headed towards Walvis Bay on the coast, passing through the Kuiseb Canyon. Namibia was not disappointing us with its vastly changing landscapes. Upon reaching the coastline of Walvis Bay, we had our first glance at the flamboyance of the famous pink flamingos. The colour was so subtle and light it almost gave the water a mirage effect of a dusk haze.

We travelled slightly north along the shore to what is called the Skeleton Coast. I had been bewildered when hearing stories of this coastline from other travellers back in previous years that had always stuck with me.

This coastline has had its fair share of names over the years. The indigenous Saan people, otherwise known as the local Bushmen, used to refer to this area as 'The Land God Made in Anger.' Later, it became known to the Portuguese sailors as 'The Gates of Hell.'

The area spans north along the coastline from Swakopmund into southern Angola. This part of the coast is inhospitable, to say the least. There is a dense ocean fog that lingers over the area most of the time, thanks to a cold ocean current with a dry and intensely hot wind coming off the dunes.

Many ships have run aground here, in a fog that encapsulates a boat and its crew within seconds. If these sailors and fishermen had made it to land, you would think that was the worst behind them. But what lies ahead are hundreds of kilometres of nothing but sand dunes rolling straight into the ocean. No trees, no water springs, and no roads.

Standing there on the sand, I could see why the Portuguese gave it the name 'The Gates of Hell.' I had heard and read stories about the ships that riddle the coastline, with the oldest dating back to the 1530s, that now lay scattered around the seashore. I looked out into the pounding surf and saw an old wreck slowly being broken up and corroded to nothing.

We spent the next few days exploring Spitzkoppe, an incredible moon-like area filled with giant boulders and granite peaks, that lay in the idle of the Namib Desert. The name Spitzkoppe is German and means 'Pointed Dome.' The rocks there are more than 120 million years old. With no other rock forms on the horizon, it was a startling sight. We found ancient petroglyphs and pictographs that were etched into this space-like rock scattered around the area.

After exploring Spitzkoppe, we pointed our bikes in the direction of Cape Town and got back onto the paved main road heading south. The near misses with speeding cars and semi-trucks were becoming overwhelming. They were not giving us any room on the roads, leaving no choice but to dive off into the shrubs that lined the shoulder. A few finger gestures after our internal steam had cooled down and we would pick the bikes up and do it all over again minutes later. I was really starting to hate the traffic. It reminded me too much of the way us Westerners drive; always in a hurry, trying to change the radio, text, make a call, turn on the AC, and never just being completely present while behind the wheel.

We had been told by white Afrikaans in Windhoek to avoid certain villages we would be riding past. They warned us, "Don't stop in those towns for water or food, and whatever you do, don't stay the night in one."

We were starting to see more often the separation of townships that are all throughout Southern Africa depending on race: white, coloured, and black townships. We made it a point to stop at every coloured and black village we passed, and those towns proved to have some of the friendliest people that we would meet on our whole journey.

In one village that we stopped at, called Rehoboth, we found a family who ran a guesthouse in the village and decided to stay for the night. This town was the main centre for the Baster people and sits on a high plateau between the Namib and Kalahari deserts.

Mac's stomach was playing up one morning, potentially from a bit of heat stroke the day before. The sudden urge to disembark her bowels was followed by the chills. Eventually, she warmed back up and continued for another hour, repeating the process all over again. We would pull over and she would quickly try to find a shrub or bush to hide behind, however, today there were a few times when nature came rumbling in her stomach and there was not a sign of a shrub or tree around, so she had no choice but to squat down on the side of the road as a truck would pass by. The stamina she showed on a day when most would just want to crawl up into a ball on a couch was a sign of true character building. Here she was, out in the scorching heat, on a no-shoulder road, having to focus on not being made into roadkill.

There always seemed to be some sort of wind blowing in Namibia. Being from Canterbury, New Zealand, a place somewhat world-renowned for its wind, it was nothing I was unfamiliar with, but cycling day-in and day-out with a headwind wasn't all that high on my list of things that I love.

We battled the ever-stronger growing headwind and reached a tiny village called Kalkand. After a couple of pedal rotations, we rolled through the rough-looking settlement. One of those towns best seen with your eyes closed. We circled back and found what looked like the only little store the town had, with locals loitering outside. I stood out in front of the shop with the bikes while Mac went inside to search for some cold drinks and food.

Soon enough, we had created a mini crowd out front, with the local youths and young males all gathering around the bikes. I made small talk with them and joked around, but in the back of my mind, I was saying, *hurry up Mac, if they wanted to, they could quite easily snatch a bike.*

Along with that inner voice came the now regular, "Give me something! Give me money!" We had grown somewhat used to these demands, which had started to happen on a daily basis again.

Lovely, I thought, as a second later another rough twenty-something male repeated once more, "Give us money!"

Hurry the fuck up, Mac! Was now on repeat in my head. As if she had read my thoughts, Mac came out of the shop, picked up on the vibe once she saw everyone gathering around the bikes, and we quickly turned around and headed back along the road. Once we were on our own for a second, we looked at the map to see if there was any sort of guesthouse in the area to spend the night.

We were shattered from the day of battling the wind and heat. Mac was still shitting liquid every so often from yesterday's heat stroke. We crossed a train track and found a nice well-built lodge hidden behind a bunch of tall trees. They were closed and had their high-security gates locked. We cycled around the back and found where the workers lived and asked if there was any chance we could pitch our tent out the back for the night.

Moments later, one of the main workers unlocked the main gate to the lodge and allowed us to pitch our tent next to the restaurant and pool. He unlocked the toilets and showers for us inside the restaurant and said to make ourselves at home.

Only minutes ago, we were being hounded to give money to the local youths, and now a polite worker had just opened up a whole lodge to two complete strangers and was allowing us to camp for free. What a stark contrast. We showered up, set up camp, and then relaxed back on the hammocks next to the pool for the evening before rolling into our tent and drifting off.

In the morning, Richard, the ever-kind worker that let us in the night before, cooked us breakfast and would not take any money for the meal or letting us stay. He said he was just happy to have been a part of our journey and wished us all the best.

Over the next few days, we kept pushing into the headwind. We would start early and try to get some kilometres on the clock before the wind gods would start the machine up, which always seemed to be around 10 a.m. Nature is a wonderful thing.

We pushed on in the late afternoon, when we

found a gap in the fencing that ran alongside the road and pushed our bikes a couple of hundred metres until we had dipped out of sight from vehicles and set up camp for the night. There was an extraordinary sunset, and we stayed up to watch the stars come out with the Milky Way on full display before retreating into our sleeping bags.

The next three days went by with—you guessed it—*more wind*. The landscape had changed to a mountainous green scattered with red rock. We were told by a local lady that it did not normally look like this, it had been years since they had had enough rain for the shrubs and plants to actually grow. It was spectacular to see the huge rusty-coloured mountains up high and the lower ground covered in shades of lush emerald shrubs. I should mention that Namibia is the driest country in Sub-Saharan Africa, so we felt pretty lucky to get to witness all this green vegetation sprouting out of the rock.

From where we camped, we had about 150 kilometres between us and the border town of Noordoewer. Now you will probably think I'm kidding, but when we woke up and noticed the wind direction, we couldn't believe our eyes. A tailwind!

We quickly packed away our camp, loaded our panniers, and set off for the border. The tailwind lasted until midday, when the winds shifted at the perfect timing for some rather large hill climbs. Namibia was not about to let us finish the country without some strong headwind.

It was not until I got a puncture in my rear tyre and we had stopped to repair it that we realised just how hot of a day it was. The breeze from our forward movement had given us the false sense that it had been cooler than it was. The needle was sitting at 45°C. I burnt my thumb just trying to put the tyre back onto the rim. After fluffing around, repairing the inner tube and putting the rear wheel back on, we were both feeling delirious from the heat. The sun pelted down on our heads and backs, sucking out any moisture from our bodies.

Whenever we reached a shaded concrete picnic spot on the side of the road, we would pull over and try to cool our bodies in the shade for ten to fifteen minutes. We would make an instant cup of warmed black coffee, have a few biscuits, put on some music and have a little morale-boosting dance before heading back out into the blazing sun.

We finally rolled down the giant hill into the valley of the river that separates Namibia and South Africa. It was like an oasis. From being higher on a plateau, we dropped down and saw lush trees, the flowing river, and to our amazement, even a flash-looking gas station with a diner attached. We plonked ourselves down inside and bought burgers and fries, washing them down with bottle after bottle of Powerade and Coca-Cola. We were dog-tired.

A truck driver stopped in, took one look at us and blurted out, "You guys haven't been out there in that furnace?"

Pointing outside, we nodded, with our faces as red as tomatoes.

"The temperature is at 47°C at the moment, and it's late afternoon—it was even hotter earlier!"

We treated ourselves to the only guesthouse on the border, both taking cold showers, and turning the air conditioning down low, we sprawled out on the bed. What a way to end in this astonishing country.

James Beatty

CHAPTER 10

Find life experiences and swallow them whole. Travel. Meet many people. Go down some dead ends and explore dark alleys. Try everything. Exhaust yourself in the glorious pursuit of life.
—Lawrence K Fish

South Africa

We woke in the morning with our body temperatures finally dropping to a normal level. We loaded our bikes up and rode to a gas station that had a diner restaurant attached and treated ourselves to a cooked breakfast and a cup of coffee. Once we felt like we were human again and fuelled by bacon and caffeine, we hopped on our bikes and rolled down to the border crossing.

This would be the last border crossing we would have to navigate on this escapade. We were stamped out of Namibia, crossed the bridge, and up to the South African border post. Now started the long, arduous process that Covid had created.

We walked into an office and were pointed towards a form that we needed to fill out. Then we were instructed to walk that form over to another smaller office and speak with a medical person who asked if we had experienced any Covid symptoms recently. Once we passed his verbal questionnaire, we were told to go to a makeshift tent outside and wait in line to get a nasal swab test. After twenty minutes of waiting, we finally had our noses punctured with a Q-tip ear swab and then had to pay in cash for the splendid experience. We then waited a further twenty minutes for the results. Then back to the office for a stamp of approval, and finally back over to the first building to hand over our passport and the results.

With a quick punch of the stamp into our passports, we were now in the last country of our ride down the continent. After all of these formalities, we were back on our bikes, but now it was 10 a.m. with the temperature already hovering over 42°C and climbing every hour!

We stopped at the only store after the border to fill up our water bottles and purchase a cold drink. I asked the shop owner what the temperature would reach today, and he replied, "Ah maybe around 46°C, she'll be warm if you two are cycling." *Thanks,* I thought to myself, *no shit!*

Once I stepped back outside, the 42°C heat instantly drained any energy that we had regained throughout the night. After dealing with heat stroke yesterday, we both found our body temperatures quickly rising and became very weary. We stood under some shade for a minute and looked at our map. Ahead of us was a two-hour climb to get out of the canyon and get back up to the plateau.

As luck would have it, the only other building in the area was a lodge next door. I said to Mac, "Let's go in and ask if we could stay for the night, if the price is right, then it's a sign that we aren't meant to cycle in this heat."

We asked the young lady at the counter, and the price she gave was about as steep as the climb we had ahead of us. After we said what we had just been doing for the past five months, the girl dropped the price by 60 percent. Now, if that's not a sign to stop cycling for the day, then I don't know what is.

We booked a room and spent the remainder of the day resting, drinking surplus amounts of fluids, and taking cold showers to help lower our body temperatures.

The next morning, we rose early and were in the saddles by 5 a.m. There was no traffic on the road, and as the sun rose for the day, we climbed out of the canyon valley.

Once we were out of the valley and on top of the plateau, we felt the wind. It was a vicious headwind that blew for the rest of the day. Picture 46°C temperatures, with a strong wind blowing in your face all day long. Imagine sticking your head in front of an oven, set on 'fan bake,' and just as you open the door to take a roast out, the heat smacks you in the face.

This is what I imagine hiking on Mars would feel like, with a heat and wind that is inescapable. Everything was hot to the touch. Our granola bars and cookies had melted to a mash, and the water in our bottles tasted like it was straight out of a freshly boiled kettle.

By late afternoon, we were both wrecked. Mac would lie down on the concrete under the shade while I would wet a bandana and drape it over her face. It was probably one of the few times that I have ever seen Mac that exhausted.

We made it to Springbok and decided to stay for a few days to fully allow our bodies to recover from the heat exhaustion. Two Belgian cyclists that we had been in touch with prior to this trip were in town. They had cycled from Belgium to South Africa. Mac had just missed them while riding through Europe months ago, since they had taken different routes, so we were looking forward to finally catching up.

Over brunch and coffee, we shared stories for hours about what the four of us had seen and experienced along our rides. They were exceptional guys and filled with character. They had mentioned that they were staying with a Warm Showers host, which is a worldwide community platform that is set up to host touring cyclists.

We rang Nicholene and Harm, who gave us their home address and told us to come on over and stay. They were some of the loveliest people that we met throughout our trip. They set us up with a room in their home and hosted a big braai gathering at their son's house where the Belgian cyclists were staying.

We had heard many stories about South Africa from cyclists up ahead, but something that they failed to mention is that South Africa is bloody hilly. During the season that we were there, the predominant wind direction blew from the south. The wind was there to greet us every morning as we would hop onto our saddles. It was draining whatever energy we had in our legs. We would find a spot to camp, set up and pass out until morning. Overnight, we seemed to regain thirty percent of our strength, which would be used in the first couple of hill climbs the following day. Then, for the rest of the day, we were forced to tap into whatever reserves we had left.

At this point, we were only five days from Cape Town. It was getting unbelievably close, but with each passing day, we still had to battle the heat and winds. At night we slept in our clammy tent, laying on top of our sleeping bags. Our physical and mental reserves were getting low, but with the end nearing, the elation was building. We had now entered the wine region just north of the Cape. It was gorgeous climbing up and looking down into the valley of wineries.

Mac had a close call with a vehicle on one of the last days while we were descending on a large downhill. A lorry had pulled over on the shoulder up ahead, which caused us to veer into the main lane of traffic. In front of us was a vehicle headed our direction in the opposite lane, but what we did not know was that behind us some wanker was planning on overtaking both us and the lorry. I passed the lorry and tucked back into the safety of the road's shoulder. While Mac was passing the lorry on her left, the wanker decided to overtake us to the right, mere inches from Mac. All of this happened while the other head-on vehicle sped towards us in the right-hand lane. It all unfolded in a nanosecond, as the passing SUV was travelling well over 120 kilometres per hour.

Such a close call had left Mac rattled. We rode a little further and found a shaded picnic spot to rest and regroup for a while. That is the thing with cycling—you are putting your life in the hands of the motorist for those seconds that they are passing you. You hope that the truck driver behind you is not on their phone and has seen you enough to move over and give you space, or that the vehicle that is merging does not cut you off. I have to say, one of the least fun things about cycling is the traffic.

Early in the mornings, we would see winery workers heading off for the day into the vineyards. There were tractors and work Utes on the roads at first light. Climbing out of a valley, I latched onto the back of one of the passing tractors, getting a free lift up the top of the hill until he pulled off towards nearby farm gates. I let go and continued gliding on for some time.

We stopped at a store to grab some lunch. While walking out scoffing into a pie, I realised my rear tyre was flat. Now, by this stage, I would like to claim we were somewhat professionals at repairing flat tyres. We had our fair share along this journey and could get the repair down to a short pit-stop worthy time.

From Piketberg, we knew we did not have far to go to reach Cape Town. We thought about pushing for a bigger day and crossing the imaginary finish line by the evening. But we decided to keep the anticipation of reaching the end last for one more night.

If there is one thing that sticks with me on long-distance adventures it's this: for the entire time you are heading north or south—or maybe it is even west to east—fixated on reaching your goal, and upon finally reaching the destination, you realise that the end was not what the trip was truly about. The real journey was everything in between that unfolded; the people that you met, the near misses, the hot and windy uphill days.

So with that, we rode out to the coast and camped out in Melkbosstrand, savouring the final moments of our voyage for one last night. We walked out to the beach and had our first glimpse of Table Mountain in the distance. We had just spent months riding towards this icon, and it now lay just on the horizon. It was a noteworthy feeling rolling into our tent that night. I could not wipe the smile from my face as I drifted to sleep.

We woke in the morning, with just thirty short kilometres to go to reach the oceanfront boardwalk of Cape Town. The five months of riding flooded through my mind. Images flew past every second, like flicking the pages of a notepad and seeing a cartoon sketch play out in front of you.

From the moment we set off in Cairo, my nostrils had been taken on a cocktail of different scents. I find when I am in remote places, I like to sit with my eyes closed for some time like an old

Buddhist monk perched on a hill, shutting down the visual overload that sometimes one can feel in a distant land, switching on my ears and nose to bring a fresh experience. Once I have left a place and if someone asks if I have been to that land, those smells and sounds are saved deep down in my memory bank. The smell of cooked horse in a camp in Kyrgyzstan or freshly baked waffles in a cafe in Belgium or the pine needles in a forest in Macedonia. Africa was no different, from the camel dung to the smell of the damp desert in the early mornings.

When moving at a glacial pace against a headwind, I found my sense of smell kick in, and I could pick up certain scents in the wind, from the pine plantations we passed in Kenya near the equator, to a chicken being barbecued over hot coals in Tanzania, to interactions with locals in a remote village, catching wafts of body odour that is almost indescribable to man. You have to experience it for yourself.

Now my nostrils were filled with the sea breeze, that irreplaceable smell of salt air when you find yourself at the coast.

We took our time as we clambered out of our tent, having done enough adventures before to know this feeling. The suspense and excitement of finishing a goal and arriving at a place you set out months ago to reach was mixed with the bittersweet emotions of knowing that this is the last time packing away the tent, stuffing it into a pannier, and riding to a town, only to be asked by locals what we are doing. There was a certain amount of pride in being able to tell them that we were riding the length of their continent.

We won't be able to say that tomorrow, I thought. *We will merely be tourists.* The locals do not seem to have the same respect when they think you have just walked off the bus alongside other tourists with dangling cameras around their necks.

But there we were, making our final breakfast and a cup of coffee next to the tent, letting it all sink in. After eating, packing and strapping everything onto the bikes, we went to ride away, when Mac noticed that her rear tyre was flat.

Off came the panniers, we flipped the bike over, patched her inner tube and pumped the tyre back up.

And away we went for a second attempt to take off for our last morning. With Table Mountain in our sights, we rode along the beach bike path most of the way from Melkbosstrand to the outskirts of Cape Town, then followed the train tracks through an industrial area where the homeless population of Cape Town had set up makeshift camps.

We were now only six kilometres from the waterfront where our journey would officially end. Stopping at a set of traffic lights, I noticed a small thorn in my front tyre. Not thinking it was lodged in that far, I yanked on the thorn to dislodge it from the rubber. Immediately after, I could hear the high-pitched sound of air shooting through the miniscule hole. My tyre deflated in seconds. I tried to keep cycling, but soon enough we had to stop to repair it. We flipped the bike over and I patched the damn tyre.

After fifteen minutes we were back on the road, counting down the kilometres and weaving our way through the city towards the waterfront. I looked down and could hardly believe my eyes, noticing that my back tyre was now flat... *c'mon* I thought, *you've got to be fuckin' kidding me! We're no more than three kilometres from the finish!*

So panniers came off, the bike flipped over, tyre off, hole found, glass removed, patched tube, tyre back on the rim, flipped the bike back over, panniers on and we were off... again.

It was at this point I could not wait to reach the end. I was just hoping my bike had the same desire as I did and would not fall apart in the final kilometres.

Before we knew it, our tyres crested the docks at the Cape Town harbour. Looking in one direction, my eyes took me straight out towards the Atlantic Ocean and the other had me looking up at Table Mountain. What a panorama to behold.

Cape Town's waterfront is one of South Africa's most tourist-dense areas. There were bars, shops, a mall and an array of high-end restaurants that scattered the dock. It was only 11 a.m. and already swarming with people like a beehive that had just been smacked.

After six months through Africa, romanticising that we would finish in solitude, embrace each other, share a kiss and shed a tear while reminiscing on what we had just experienced… well, no, it wasn't going to be like that, not here.

We hopped off our bikes and wheeled them over to an enormous yellow picture frame monument mounted on the dock with Table Mountain as the backdrop for the camera-wielding sightseers to get their photos taken.

I asked a woman walking by if she would not mind taking our photo. We hugged and smiled while posing for the camera.

The lady then asked, "Where did you guys come from?"

I puffed out my chest and thought, *ah yes, here we go, someone I can finally tell what we have just done.*

I exclaimed, "We just rode from Egypt!"

Her response was instant, "Oh yeah, I just flew from England yesterday," as she handed our camera back.

Abruptly my bubble had been popped, in one of those wonderfully ego-deflating moments we have all experienced at least once. Mac and I laughed at each other. We knew that is what we needed to hear.

There was a sense of pride that hit me just in that moment as we finished, followed by a vast amount of jubilation that flooded my system as we rolled our bikes over to a nearby cafe. We had ridden these steel-framed, two-wheeled contraptions 11,000 kilometres in six months and through ten countries. We crossed through a military coup, rode past wild animals, navigated around countries at war, and swept through villages that have hardly changed since David Livingstone's days.

As we sat in those cafe seats, the people passing by saw two sun-scorched, tattered-clothed, tired-looking souls and absolutely nobody there knew what we had just completed.

But in all of that lies the secret. We do not go on these expeditions for the applause of others. We do them for ourselves. Deep down, we did not care that no one knew where we had just come from months earlier. We did not want claps and cheers.

We enjoy the challenges that lie in between the start and finish and the moments that no one gets to see apart from the people partaking in the journey. The interactions with locals, the storms, flat tyres, intense heat, viscous winds, and the generosity of complete strangers—this is why we do these adventures.

What a ride it had been.

The end.

The Road South

Life is a dance, if we're not smiling each day and two-stepping with pure freedom, then I'm afraid we might have gotten it all wrong. Do we really think that we are here to wake up feeling exhausted, force-feed ourselves and drive to work to chase six figures in the hopes of enjoying a few years at the end of our lives? Do we go to a concert only to hear the final note of the last song? No! We go to dance through the whole damn thing. We never even think about the end of the show. Why do that in our lives? So smile, and dance the day away. If you're somewhere you're not happy, change it. Don't wait to listen to the last song. Enjoy the dance!

—James Beatty

James Beatty

ABOUT THE AUTHOR

James Beatty has travelled around the world for the last decade, visiting over 100 countries and six continents by means of bicycle, walking, hitchhiking, trains and planes to far-off countries.

Originally from New Zealand, James set out at the age of twenty-two to see the world. Over the years that followed, he has walked the length of New Zealand, from Mexico to Canada, in the High Andes, and all over the Himalayas. James hitchhiked across North America, Europe, and Australia, and overlanded the length of the Americas, starting from Ushuaia, Argentina. His latest adventure was cycling the length of Africa, from Cairo to Cape Town.

When not travelling, James can be found in libraries and secondhand book shops, poring over old, tattered maps and planning his next adventure.

The Road South is his first book. Stay tuned for more books to come.

James Beatty

The Road South

James Beatty